PASSION PL

Pam Dodds

Peter Nichols

PASSION PLAY

EYRE METHUEN · LONDON

Passion Play was first published in 1981 by Eyre Methuen Ltd.,
11 New Fetter Lane, London EC4P 4EE
Second, post-production edition 1981
Copyright © 1981 by Peter Nichols

ISBN 0 413 47910 2 (Hardback)
     0 413 47800 9 (Paperback)

Set in IBM 10pt Journal by ⊼ Tek-Art, Croydon, Surrey
Printed in Great Britain by Fakenham Press Ltd, Fakenham,
Norfolk.

Passion Play was first performed by the Royal Shakespeare Company at the Aldwych Theare, London, on 8th January 1981 (press night 13th January), with the following cast:

AGNES, 50	Priscilla Morgan
ELEANOR, 45	Billie Whitelaw
JAMES, 50	Benjamin Whitrow
JIM, 50	Anton Rodgers
KATE, 25	Louise Jameson
NELL, 45	Eileen Atkins

A number of others (at least six) who do not speak dialogue. They play waiters, assistants, a doctor, diners, guests at Private Views, etc.

Directed by Mike Ockrent.

The set resembles (and at times represents) a fashionable art gallery. It includes a flight of stairs and is on two levels.

At the time of going to press a West End production of *Passion Play,* with Albert Finney as Jim, was planned to open on 8 December 1981.

Act One

A living room. ELEANOR, JAMES and KATE are seated, drinking from coffee cups and glasses. KATE is smoking. Someone has just finished speaking.

Silence. She puts out her cigarette. JAMES breathes in sharply, covers his mouth. ELEANOR drains her glass. A clock chimes the first half.

KATE. What's that? Midnight already?

JAMES. Half past.

KATE. No! My watch must have stopped. Christ. Sorry.

ELEANOR. Whatever for?

KATE. I'd no idea. No wonder James was yawning.

JAMES. Was I?

ELEANOR. He's always yawning.

KATE. I must go.

JAMES. At my age I nod off so easily.

ELEANOR. At your age? You've always been a yawner.

JAMES. A yawner possibly.

ELEANOR. All our married life.

JAMES. I've never been in the habit of nodding off before. Not like now, at the drop of a hat.

ELEANOR. You've always needed at least eight hours.

JAMES. There's no place like bed.

KATE. Right.

ELEANOR. We're all agreed on that.

KATE. And I must let you get to yours. I didn't mean to stay so long.

ELEANOR. You're mad, we love people dropping in. They rarely do, we're so far out up here. It's a very quiet life.

KATE. In that case I'll come more often.

ELEANOR. We'd love that. Shouldn't we, James?

JAMES (*yawning*). Absolutely.

The WOMEN *laugh.*

Forgive me. (*He stands.*) Let's kill this, shall we, before you go? (*He pours wine for them all.*)

ELEANOR. You have been able to help her then?

JAMES. Not yet. Kate's told me what she's after. I'll be what use I can, which isn't much, I'm afraid. My field's so limited. Strictly the Art Game.

ELEANOR (*to* KATE): But you knew that, didn't you?

KATE. Right. That's all I want. As I told him while you were with your student. It was you and your stories of the Arab sheikhs and their art collections gave me the idea in the first place. Then Albert suggested I take in other fields — football, architecture, armaments, medicine — the whole crazy relationship between Arab dollars and British know-how.

ELEANOR. Fascinating subject.

JAMES. Absolutely.

KATE. Almost the last thing Albert did was to get the publishers to commission this book. I owe it to his memory to complete it.

ELEANOR. You're doing both text *and* illustrations?

KATE. Right. And I want to interview the wives as well. You, for instance.

ELEANOR. I didn't see much. As soon as we got to the palace, I had to go and sit in the women's apartments.

KATE. The seraglio. Well, there you are. To people like us living in a sort of run-down monogamy, that whole harem scene is very sexy.

ELEANOR. They're just fashionable girls with Gucci handbags. They may have gone to the Sorbonne but we still got the cold mutton after the men had had their fill.

KATE. Why struggle, James? Just let it come.

JAMES (*yawning*). God, I'm sorry.

KATE (*rises*). I'd better go.

He kisses her on the cheek.

JAMES. I'll send you on a list of names.

KATE. Great. Really. And sometime soon an hour's chat? With a tape recorder? Both of you?

ELEANOR. We're always here.

JAMES. Almost always.

ELEANOR. You know our number.

KATE. Right.

ELEANOR and KATE go to the hall. JAMES stays in the room, clearing glasses and putting KATE's empty cigarette packet into the ashtray.

ELEANOR and KATE stay in the hall. ELEANOR helps KATE with her outdoor clothing. They talk but their dialogue is drowned by a sudden, fortissimo burst of choral music. Mozart's Requiem: from 'Dies Irae' to 'Stricte discussurus'.

By the time it's over, KATE has gone by the front door and ELEANOR has returned to JAMES in the living-room. The music ends as suddenly as it began.

JAMES. I thought she'd never go.

ELEANOR. That was obvious.

JAMES. Well, nearly quarter to one —

ELEANOR. *I'd* be in no hurry either. Back to an empty flat, a lonely bed. I don't know how she can stay on there, with so many memories of Albert.

JAMES. *She's* not much more than a memory of Albert. Everything she's got is his — phrases, gestures, points of view. Like a ghost.

ELEANOR. What chance has she had to be anything else? Five years with Albert *I'd* be a ghost.

JAMES. I doubt it. She was no-one to *start* with.

ELEANOR. I happen to like her.

JAMES. I don't *mind* her.

ELEANOR. You made her feel about this small.

JAMES. How d'you know what she felt?

ELEANOR. She told me.

JAMES. No.

ELEANOR. In the hall, just now. I think you might have made an effort.

JAMES. I *was* making an effort.

He turns out some of the lights.

ELEANOR. It cost her a lot to ask that favour but you left her feeling about this small.

JAMES. As you said before.

ELEANOR. Why is it you never like my girl-friends?

JAMES. Kate's one of you girl-friends, is she?

ELEANOR. Why not?

JAMES. Isn't she a bit young?

ELEANOR. She was even younger for Albert. Eighteen when they first met. And he was forty-something.

JAMES. That was the point. For *him.* The flattery of youth. He could make it with a chick.

ELEANOR. I enjoy young people's company.

JAMES. She's about the same age as our daughters. You never much enjoy theirs.

ELEANOR. Same as Janet, older than Ruth.

JAMES. And you didn't crave *their* company.

ELEANOR. *I enjoyed it.* Anyway, Ruth and Janet have gone now, they've got their husbands to look to. And daughters are different. I'm not Kate's mother.

JAMES. You could be.

ELEANOR. What?

JAMES. You're old enough.

ELEANOR. Yes, but I'm not. I talk to her in a way I never could with the girls.

JAMES. Really? What about?

ELEANOR. Men. Sex. Love. She very much reminds me of myself when I was her age.

JAMES. Seriously?

ELEANOR. Can't you see the resemblance?

JAMES. You were a working-class drop-out on the run from a provincial suburb. Kate's a stockbroker's daughter, middle-class, knows the score —

ELEANOR. That doesn't matter. We're both looking for a brighter world, we go for the same kind of men —

JAMES. Albert?

ELEANOR. Not Albert. You. (*He looks at her.*) She told me when we went to make the coffee. She finds you a very attractive man. So there's your chance.

JAMES. If only I found her an attractive woman.

ELEANOR. You make that very obvious. Which must be quite a challenge to a girl like her. She's used to getting her own way. I was the same. I can read her like a book.

JAMES. Then you don't think she *does* find me attractive?

ELEANOR. I'm sure she does. She means nothing by it, though. Otherwise why tell *me*?

JAMES. Of course. I see that.

ELEANOR. But I was clearly meant to pass it on, so I have.

JAMES. Very generous.

ELEANOR. I like to see you happy.

JAMES. Knowing she doesn't interest me.

ELEANOR. And also that, even if she did, an approach like that would only send you pelting for cover.

She leaves the room with the glasses, etc. She goes through the kitchen and off. He follows her, calling:

JAMES. Don't be too sure! The right offer, on the right day, from the right woman, I've already warned you, someone with my lack of experience would be mad not to grab with both hands.

He bolts the front door. She returns and they move through the hall together towards the stairs.

ELEANOR. I'm sick of hearing this. You had as much as most men. Certainly as many chances.

JAMES. In our day you could never be sure. Girls' behaviour then was criminal. There seemed to be so little action, it's a wonder the race survived.

ELEANOR. Quite a few girls tried the direct approach with you.

JAMES. Who, for instance?

ELEANOR. God, I can't remember now. It's nearly thirty years ago.

JAMES. Do you mean when we were at art school?

ELEANOR. Half the girls in the dressmaking department fell over themselves to attract you but you never noticed.

JAMES. I don't wonder, it came so seldom. *You* never tried the direct approach.

ELEANOR. I learnt from the others, I waited for you to come to me.

JAMES. You could afford to. (*He embraces and kisses her.*) You were the most attractive. Still are.

She avoids his advances and starts to climb the stairs.

No amount of coming out with it could ever be a match for you. Sitting there like a cat with cream, knowing you had them all beat hollow. Smug's the word for that.

He catches up and begins making love.

Aren't you, eh, a cat with cream?

ELEANOR. What *are* you doing?

JAMES. Smug as hell. A girl like Kate can even tell you I interest her because of course she knows she's safe. She knows I'm yawning for her to leave so that you and I can go upstairs.

ELEANOR. *Halfway* upstairs?

JAMES. Why not? Now the girls have gone? We're all alone. No-one's going to appear on the landing and ask us what we're doing.

ELEANOR. It's many a year since they did that.

JAMES. And many a year since we did this.

ELEANOR. You'll put my back out.

JAMES. The top stair then. With the flat landing?

ELEANOR. James! I'm a grandmother. You're a grandfather. There's a place for that kind of thing. (*She frees herself.*) It's called the bedroom.

She climbs to the top, opens the door there and goes off by it. He follows, turns off all the lights and goes off too, closing the door.

The 'Dies Irae' bursts out again.

A restaurant. KATE sits alone, smoking, with a drink. Behind her, a table where two WOMEN sit talking and drinking coffee.

A WAITER *replaces* KATE's *drink with another, smiles at her and speaks. She thanks him, finishes the last and hands him the glass. He leans over her and speaks. She listens, smiling. The* WAITER *leads her to a vacated table and she sits. He lays a napkin in her lap.* JAMES *arrives and the music ends.*

KATE. Hullo.

JAMES. God, I'm sorry.

KATE. Don't be.

He sits beside her. Mutter of conversation and sounds of knives and forks.

JAMES. I thought you'd be gone. This Lebanese curator talks the hind legs off a donkey.

KATE. It's all right.

JAMES. I thought —

KATE. You're here. That's all that matters. (*Offers her cheek to be kissed, he does.*) I'd already scored with the waiter.

JAMES. You've got a drink?

KATE. My third.

The WAITER *approaches, stands by.*

JAMES. I'm usually so punctual.

KATE. I'm not, I warn you. Just today. Serves me right for being too eager.

JAMES. Cinzano Bianco, please.

The WAITER *goes.* JAMES *looks at the menu.*

Have you ordered anything to eat?

KATE. I can't think about food. Too excited. Too many butterflies. It's been like that ever since you called.

JAMES. That seems disproportionate. I only want to suggest some other people you might interview for your book.

KATE. Is that all? Right. I thought perhaps you'd received my message?

JAMES. Message?

KATE. I sent a message through your wife. She didn't pass it on?

JAMES. I don't think so.

KATE. Unexpected. (*She shrugs*.) She can't be as confident as she looks.

JAMES. Oh. If you mean about being fond of me — ?

KATE. Finding you attractive.

JAMES. That's it, yes, she told me that, yes, very flattering for a man of my age. Yes, she did. Thanks.

KATE. I like older men.

JAMES. Well, obviously. Albert was my age exactly.

KATE. D'you know he admired you more than anyone?

JAMES. That much? We were close friends certainly, over thirty years, but he had such a brilliant career, all get-up-and-go, by comparison I must have seemed a stick.

KATE. One of his strengths as an editor was he recognised the real stuff when he saw it. He made me watch you closely. Your modesty fascinated him. *The* man in his field, he used to say, no contenders.

JAMES. Well, restoring modern art is not that wide a field, you know. More like a kitchen garden.

KATE. Never shows off. Doesn't need to. That's a man in total control of himself. Nobody's ever disturbed his equilibrium. Watch him closely. So I did.

The WAITER *returns with* JAMES's *drink, sets it before him, leaning over.* KATE *does not alter her voice.*

And that's how I came to realise you're one of the most desirable men I've ever met.

JAMES *looks up at the* WAITER.

JAMES. Thank you.

KATE. Almost painfully so. You must have noticed.

JAMES. Would you like some Vichyssoise? Gazpacho? A little salmon?

KATE. Anything light, I don't mind.

JAMES (*ordering*): Two Vichyssoise, fresh salmon for the lady, and for me escalopes provençales. (*To* KATE:) Soave to drink? (*She nods.*) Thanks.

The WAITER *writes and goes with the menus.*

KATE. I'm sorry if my interest was ever an embarrassment.

JAMES. Never. No. Except perhaps with that waiter —

KATE. It must have been so obvious at times. Though I tried not to let it show.

JAMES. I honestly didn't notice.

KATE. Come on —

JAMES. Never occurred to me.

KATE. Amazing.

JAMES. You were Albert's girl. Taboo.

KATE. Right. I didn't dare move while he was alive and as we never meet without your wife I thought the best approach was through her.

JAMES. Eleanor assumed you only flattered me to use my connections. Luckily.

KATE. She was meant to.

JAMES. I did myself.

KATE. My cover-up job was too effective.

JAMES. *Do* myself. I must admit.

KATE (*her hand on his*). Forget that now.

JAMES. The only time I thought of you like that was at the funeral.

KATE. I *chose* that dress for you.

JAMES. Dress?

KATE. Purple silk. Cost the earth.

JAMES. I didn't notice the dress. No, I meant that suddenly

seeing you as Albert's — what shall I call you — common-law widow?

KATE. Right. There's no word for what I am.

JAMES. Well, seeing you then, among his middle-aged friends, I realised how young you were. Even younger than Albert's daughter. And I couldn't help but see the way some of Albert's mates consoled you.

KATE. Right! The friends who'd been the last to accept me as his lover were the first to try to undress me as his widow.

JAMES. I remarked on that to Eleanor.

KATE. I didn't *mind*. Being suddenly available is quite arousing. The ultimate sexual threat. The other wives were very much aware. And I knew *you* were watching. Which was nice too.

JAMES. I wasn't watching. I *noticed*.

She smiles, finishes her gin. The WAITER *serves food.*

The lights fade slightly on the restaurant set and come up fully on the living-room, where ELEANOR *enters from the kitchen door with* AGNES. *They go into the living-room. They bring mugs of coffee.*

AGNES. You noticed that, did you?

ELEANOR. Not till James remarked on it.

AGNES. Their hands were everywhere. God Almighty, I thought, you smutty little trollop.

ELEANOR. I'm not sure you can blame Kate for that.

AGNES. I can blame her for wearing a purple silk creation that must have cost my husband more than he ever spent on a dress for me. And scent you could have cut with a scythe. I blame her for rushing along that very morning to have an expensive hair-do.

ELEANOR. You don't *know* that, Agnes.

AGNES. I know how it looks without, my dear.

ELEANOR. She was only being the good hostess. Which is what she's chiefly known for.

AGNES. What she's chiefly known for is stealing other people's husbands.

ELEANOR. Only once.

AGNES. Once! You don't imagine that was the first time those old mates had felt her up?

ELEANOR. I thought so, yes.

AGNES. She might at least have fought off their drunken fingers till after the funeral. With our sons and daughters there and Albert's parents and brother and sister and all their families —

ELEANOR. Kate's people didn't come?

AGNES. They've never approved. Her father didn't relish the thought of a son-in-law older than himself. Calling him 'dad'.

The lights favour JAMES *and* KATE.

KATE. I can't manage any more.

JAMES. You've eaten nothing.

KATE. My heart's in my mouth. I can hardly breathe. Can you?

JAMES. Shall I order coffee?

KATE. No. There's coffee at my place.

JAMES. That's out of the question, Kate. There's a painting I told I Eleanor I must leave in Bond Street and as you know my home's half an hour's drive at least —

KATE. I can do it in fifteen minutes.

JAMES. I remember your driving, yes.

KATE. I didn't mean the drive.

She takes his hand and kisses it.

JAMES. She'd wonder where I'd been.

KATE. So she doesn't know we're meeting?

JAMES. I told her I'd be eating with the Lebanese curator —

KATE. Two alibis? Not clever. It looks fishy. You get sussed out.

JAMES. But I could say I'd met you and given you a few more names.

He hands her an envelope.

KATE. Three alibis? And you didn't know I was interested? Well, it's all true so far.

JAMES. Would you rather she knew? You don't care?

KATE (*shrugs*). Why should I, if you can't come back for coffee?

JAMES. No reason.

KATE. None at all.

JAMES. I'll probably tell her then.

KATE. Do.

JAMES. D'you want coffee here?

KATE. Mine's better.

JAMES. I'm sure.

KATE. I'd put my mouth in shape for that. I may have some alone, thinking of you. But it won't be the same.

JAMES *beckons to the* WAITER.

In the living-room, ELEANOR *is still moving and* AGNES *is still.*

ELEANOR. I hesitate to say this, Agnes, but if close friends can't who can? Please don't misunderstand. I'm only saying what I hope will bring you peace of mind. I'm sorry to hear you still going on, that's all.

AGNES. Going on?

ELEANOR. About Albert and Kate. I'd hoped now he's dead, you'd find the generosity to forget what happened. Well, forgive anyway. Your new friend's such a pleasant man, your life's taken a fresh direction, it's full of promise, surely there's no need to keep those old animosities alive?

Pause. She looks straight at AGNES, *who pointedly waits as though for the end of a sermon.*

AGNES. My new friend and I have both been through the wars

and without each other we might never have picked up the pieces again. But what makes you believe he could ever in a million years make up for the loss of my husband? And I don't mean his death. I mean the loss while he was alive! Haven't you even grasped that Albert was my life? We not only had four children, we made his career. Together. Coming from a semi-literate home, he longed for mass enlightenment. He lusted to cast light. In another age perhaps he'd have drafted constitutions, fought as the barricades. In ours he became a crusading editor, he influenced the finest minds of his generation. And finally threw all that away to satisfy an itching cock.

ELEANOR. Well, not entirely, Agnes —

AGNES. Then you tell me to forgive and forget?

ELEANOR. I mean, he did continue to function after he went to live with Kate —

AGNES. Forgive that bitch? What for?

ELEANOR. For *your* sake. Your peace of mind.

JAMES *has paid the bill and he and* KATE *are leaving their table and making across the upper level to the stairs. The* WAITER *clears, light goes on him.*

AGNES. Don't waste your sympathy on me, dear. I've got a little man takes care of that.

ELEANOR. Then for the sake of your friends —

AGNES. What friends?

ELEANOR. Your many old friends —

AGNES. He took most of them with him. Eventually. She won them over.

ELEANOR. *We're* still your friends.

AGNES. James never liked me.

ELEANOR. Not true. Believe me, there are more than you think. And we none of us like seeing you in this bitter state —

AGNES. Oh, don't you 'like' it? Oh, how sad!

ELEANOR. It's boring to listen to, frankly.

AGNES. It doesn't bore me. Christ, no! It keeps me alive. I'll see her in the poorhouse. Or perhaps the whorehouse would suit her better.

JAMES and KATE have come down the stairs and turn into the hall space.

KATE. Thanks for lunch, if nothing else.

JAMES. Thank you for coming.

AGNES. I'll take back everything he gave her.

KATE. You must taste my coffee some time.

AGNES. Every lemon squeezer.

KATE. Sometime soon.

JAMES. I'd like that, yes, but I can seldom get away from home.

AGNES. Everything she didn't buy.

KATE. It's time you did.

AGNES (*smiling*). He never married, did he?

JAMES. Perhaps it is.

KATE stands close, pressing her body against his.

AGNES. Five years he lived with her but never married her.

ELEANOR. Kate wouldn't have him. She values her freedom.

AGNES. I'll fight her till I drop.

KATE. Please try, won't you?

ELEANOR. You'll lose your friends.

AGNES. I can manage without.

KATE. You know where I am. Just ring.

She kisses JAMES on the mouth, lingeringly.

AGNES. This is more important than pleasing friends. This is fighting evil, which he did too as long as he could spot it.

The kiss ends.

KATE. Next time we'll have the coffee first. Only eat when we've worked up an appetite.

She turns to go.

JAMES. I'll give your love to Eleanor.

He goes off the other way.

AGNES. You can only tell me to forgive because you haven't the vaguest idea how this experience *feels*.

ELEANOR. I suppose that's true. James and I have been unusually lucky. Our daughters used to complain we were getting dull.

AGNES. Well —

ELEANOR. Really?

AGNES. A bit.

ELEANOR. D'you think so?

AGNES. You never surprise us.

ELEANOR. Sometimes we'd have welcomed a dash of danger.

AGNES. It's how to stop it once you've started.

ELEANOR. But somehow we seem to be a naturally monogamous pair.

AGNES. Who isn't? Who doesn't believe it's made in heaven?

ELEANOR. We don't think *that*. We're not romantic. My opinion is most couples come to grief through expecting too much of each other.

AGNES. But how can you bear the miseries, unless you expect the glories too?

ELEANOR. There's hardly time enough in the day for all the work and music and family and fornication, leave alone the glory!

AGNES *has been preparing to leave. They now make for the hall.*

AGNES. Wait till one of you feels the itch —

ELEANOR. Not everyone does.

The front door opens and JAMES *enters.*

Oh, hullo, love.

JAMES. Agnes! How good to see you! I was afraid you might have gone.

AGNES. I'm just on my way.

They kiss. ELEANOR *stands by.*

You smell sexy. Nice after-shave.

JAMES. Why are you rushing off like this?

AGNES. I'm meeting my fellow at half-past three and isn't it getting on for that now?

JAMES. Ten past.

ELEANOR. Where on earth have you been till now?

JIM *enters at the cupboard, dressed the same as* JAMES. *No-one acknowledges him.*

JIM. The traffic. We agreed the traffic.

JAMES. The traffic.

AGNES. Oh, God, is it bad?

JAMES. Friday afternoon?

AGNES. Must dash. Bye-bye.

ELEANOR. Let's go shopping some time, shall we?

They kiss.
The men watch.

JIM. Better *tell* her. I want to tell her.

AGNES. I don't get that much time.

JIM. Good excuse not to mention Kate till Agnes went —

ELEANOR. Just an hour or two.

JIM. I *want* to tell her.

AGNES. I'll try.

JIM. Not everything.

AGNES. Goodbye James.

JAMES. Bye-bye.

AGNES goes. ELEANOR closes the door.

JIM. Not about the kiss, for instance.

ELEANOR. Hullo, my love. ·

She embraces and kisses him.

JIM. In the restaurant, the whole length of her body against mine —

ELEANOR. I've missed you.

JAMES. Have you?

JIM — her tongue straight to the back of my mouth, circling like a snake inside —

ELEANOR. Haven't you missed me?

JAMES. I always miss you.

JIM. The almost forgotten feel of an unknown woman —

ELEANOR. Agnes was right. You reek of perfume.

JIM. Christ!

JAMES. Do I?

ELEANOR. *Is* it aftershave?

JIM. She *knows* your aftershave.

ELEANOR. I don't think so.

JAMES. I've no idea.

ELEANOR. Smells more like women's perfume.

JIM. The dealer. Magda.

JAMES. Oh, in the gallery, yes, this dragon was wearing some kind of knock-out drops, I remember.

ELEANOR. It *smells* like Bond Street.

JAMES. What does Bond Street smell like?

ELEANOR. Expensive tarts.

JAMES. What do you know about expensive tarts?

ELEANOR. Not much.

JAMES. They liked my work on the painting.

ELEANOR. Which was that?

JAMES. The Frank Stella.

ELEANOR. They must have kept you hanging about.

They have now returned to the living-room.

JIM. No. She can easily catch you out there.

JAMES. Not long, no.

JIM. *Talk* more. You usually talk more, don't you? Simply say you had some lunch with Kate, gave her the list of names and —

ELEANOR. Did you have a drink at the gallery?

JAMES. No.

ELEANOR. Not white wine? You haven't drunk white wine?

JAMES. No.

ELEANOR. I thought I tasted it when you kissed me.

JIM. Lunch.

JAMES. That was lunch.

JIM. With Kate.

JAMES. With the Lebanese curator.

JIM. Kate!

JAMES. He wants me to buy more post-impressionists and sixties British for his sheiks and emirs.

JIM. And you met Kate for a drink nearby —

JAMES. It's a profitable sideline buying for the Gulf.

ELEANOR. Yes, indeed.

JIM. Why are you doing this? To hide the fact you've eaten lunch with an attractive girl who doesn't attract you?

ELEANOR. Arabs don't drink, do they?

JIM. Christ! Orange!

JAMES. Orange juice. I had the wine.

JIM. Still not too late to say you met for a drink —

JAMES. Agnes looked rather well, I thought.

ELEANOR. We had a nasty scene.

JAMES. Oh, dear.

He is absently moving about. She is correcting a score.

JIM. But you're right, she wouldn't understand —

ELEANOR. If you'd been sooner, it wouldn't have happened.

JAMES. Sorry about that.

JIM. And anyway you don't *want* to tell her. Don't *want* to finish it there, do you?

JAMES. What was your disagreement about?

JIM. You feel alive.

ELEANOR. Oh, Kate, Kate, Kate, what else?

JIM (*to her*): I've just had lunch with Kate.

ELEANOR. She never talks of anything else.

JIM. Except that neither of us could eat.

ELEANOR. And I'm afraid I told her so.

JIM. Her tongue's been in my mouth.

ELEANOR. I told her it was boring.

JAMES. No wonder you had a disagreement.

JIM. She's not pretty, Eleanor.

ELEANOR. Well, she was so vindictive.

JIM. Not nearly as pretty as you. But different. More flagrant.

JAMES. Even now that Albert's dead? What can she do?

JIM. Kate doesn't care who's watching.

ELEANOR. She wants everything back. Every single thing he bought her. I found myself defending Kate. I've decided I like her better.

JIM (*to her*): I love you, Eleanor. But she's exciting.

JAMES. Should we tell her, d'you think?

JIM. She's dangerous.

ELEANOR. Tell who? Kate?

JAMES. Yes. Warn her.

ELEANOR. She can look after herself.

JAMES. Absolutely.

JIM. Anyone could have seen that kiss.

ELEANOR. Intruders get caught in the crossfire.

JIM. Though I suppose it wouldn't *look* much to a passer-by?

JAMES. D'you feel like a little nap?

JIM. An affectionate goodbye at most.

JAMES (*embracing her*). An afternoon lie-down?

JIM. No more.

ELEANOR. I'm giving a lesson in fifteen minutes.

JIM. A passer-by couldn't have seen the tongue.

JAMES. How long for?

ELEANOR. An hour.

JAMES. And then?

ELEANOR. And then we're rehearsing Verdi's Requiem for the Albert Hall and what you call a little nap always requires a long nap afterwards.

She has her score and moves to the hall, JAMES *and* JIM *following.*

I don't want to repeat the occasion I was singled out from the other sopranos for yawning in the Sanctus. How about tonight?

JAMES. You know very well afternoons are best.

ELEANOR. Tomorrow afternoon then.

JAMES. All right. Tonight.

ELEANOR (*laughing*). Whatever's the matter with you suddenly? While I'm teaching have a cold bath. Or go for a run.

JAMES. I might do that.

She takes the score off to the music-room upstage of the living-room. JAMES stays in the hall. JIM goes to the cubicle representing the phone-booth. He dials, waits. JAMES calls off to ELEANOR.

Are you sure you're free tomorrow afternoon?

Lights up on KATE's room: couch, chair, low lighting. A phone on the floor is ringing. KATE enters wearing only a slip-on gown, smoking a cigarette. She kneels to answer.

KATE. Yeah?

JIM puts his money in. Sounds of the tone until he does. ELEANOR comes from the music-room.

ELEANOR. What?

JAMES. Are you free tomorrow afternoon?

ELEANOR. One student in the morning. Afternoon quite free.

JIM. Hullo? Kate?

KATE. Yeah.

JIM. James Croxley here.

ELEANOR. Shall I book you in? (*She goes to the foot of the stairs.*)

KATE. Hullo. How are you? (*She lies on the couch, resting the receiver on her stomach.*)

JAMES. And no choir rehearsal?

ELEANOR. Not till Saturday.

JIM. I was a bit late home and Eleanor wondered where I'd been.

JAMES. I'll keep you to that.

KATE. So you told her. What did she say?

JIM. I didn't, no —

KATE. I see —

JIM. Well, Agnes was there and I thought —

KATE. Agnes? She'd have suspected all kinds of wild things that I'm sad to say never happened.

ELEANOR (*to* JAMES, *who is following her up the stairs*): Where are you going now?

JIM. Yes.

JAMES. To put my running-shoes on.

JIM. And wasted no time suggesting them to Eleanor.

KATE. Right. A very heavy scene.

ELEANOR. You won't be coming Saturday?

JAMES. Isn't it being broadcast live?

ELEANOR. Yes.

JIM. They both smelt your perfume on me.

KATE. Poor James.

JAMES. I'll listen at home. You won't mind?

She precedes him into the bedroom. He shuts the door behind them.

KATE. What did you say? About the perfume?

JIM. I said it was someone else's?

KATE. Someone else's?

JIM. The Bond Street dealer's.

KATE. I suppose you're pretty nifty on your feet.

JIM. How d'you mean?

KATE. Used to dealing with narrow scrapes?

JIM. Me?

KATE. You must be.

JIM. Not at all.

KATE. Did she believe you?

JIM. Yes, I think so. I was going to say I'd lunched with you but by the time Agnes had gone, the moment seemed to have passed. So can I ask you not to mention it?

KATE. I wasn't going to.

JIM. No, I'm sure.

KATE. You sound as breathless as I feel.

JIM. I've been jogging round the park. I've no more coins so I can't talk long. There's something you should be warned about. Would you care to come to dinner with us here? Next week?

KATE. Warned about? What?

JIM. Otherwise on Saturday night, if you're not busy, I could drop in at your place . . .

The 'Agnus Dei' from Verdi's Requiem, sudden and loud.

JIM and KATE continue for some moments unheard, then lights fade on JIM as he replaces the telephone. KATE puts hers down too and continues lying on the settee, smoking.

The lights change on her room to show more. JAMES enters, wearing shirt, trousers, no shoes or socks, drinking coffee from a cup. JIM walks over to join them, sits in the spare chair. For some time they listen to the music.

JAMES sits on the settee. In moving to make room, KATE lets her gown slip and JAMES caresses her legs. Then he kisses her. Then he resumes drinking.

JAMES. This is the 'Agnus Dei'. I'll have to be going soon. There's only the 'Lux Eterna' and the Libera Me' to come.

KATE. How long does it take her from the Albert Hall?

JAMES. She gets a lift with one of the contraltos. A slow and careful driver who likes to hang about chatting afterwards.

KATE. You're all right, then.

JAMES. But not for long.

She goes to the tuner, turns down the volume.

KATE. Time to help yourself to another drop. It's simmering.

JIM. What does she *want*?

JAMES. No. Really.

KATE. You said you like the way I make it. Hot and strong.

They smile at each other.

JIM. Not just *me* surely?

KATE (*moving*). Well, you know where to find it. If you want it.

JIM (*to* KATE): You've had the list of names, the introductions.

KATE. I hope you think it was worth waiting for.

JAMES. Absolutely.

JIM. Well —

JAMES. I'm surprised you need to ask —

JIM. But since you did it wasn't, no —

JAMES. And thank you —

JIM. Wasn't worth the lying and fear and risk of discovery, no —

KATE. Thank *you*. It's been quite a while for me.

JIM. I don't believe you.

KATE. I went a bit mad after Albert died but I've calmed down since.

JAMES. Did anyone stay the night of the funeral?

KATE. I'm not giving names.

JAMES. I wasn't asking.

KATE. I told you I wore that dress for you. I wanted you so much I nearly creamed myself. Couldn't face bed alone that night. The thrill of the new-found freedom wore off after a week or so. I've been behaving myself for at least a month now. Which is good. I need to be steady to start my new life. But by the time you rang I was fairly desperate.

JIM. A man of fifty? You must have been.

KATE. And the lunch turned out to be just lunch so you can imagine that tonight, after I'd bathed and washed away all traces of scent—

JAMES. I realised you weren't wearing any. Thoughtful.

JIM. I missed that scent.

KATE. And after that put on the simple blouse and skirt and you tuned in to the Requiem, I felt like some kind of vestal virgin. So if I was quick to come, you know the reason —

JAMES. I was afraid you found me slow.

JIM. I nearly failed. For the first time since —

KATE. Slow's best. Though quick's good sometimes too. Exciting and flattering.

JAMES. You didn't wear any underclothes.

KATE. I know you like the wholesome approach. Eleanor and I went shopping together and I was buying the sort of lingerie Albert liked. Black lacy satin, belts and suspenders. And Eleanor said you hated all that.

JIM. On her, yes.

KATE. You liked the back-to-nature style.

JAMES. I always assumed Albert did as well.

KATE. Maybe with Agnes.

JIM. A lover's different.

KATE. When we first met, when I was eighteen, he bought me several sets. He found it very arousing.

JAMES. I thought I knew him well.

KATE. He couldn't resist me in the changing cubicle. With all the assistants outside, we had it standing up.

JIM (*amazed*): There isn't anything she won't do!

KATE. Reflected in several mirrors. (*She laughs.*)

JAMES. Talk about a dark horse.

KATE. He loved all that. He'd ring sometimes from the office, say at three in the afternoon and I'd have to get up in all this stuff —

JIM. Perhaps because your body's not attractive enough without —

KATE. And sometimes he wouldn't arrive and I'd be sitting there hours on end feeling really stupid, in black stockings, reeking of scent —

JIM. Without the knocking-shop accoutrements, you're far from irresistible —

JAMES. D'you mean he did it on purpose?

KATE. No. He couldn't get away, that's all.

JIM. Thank God it wasn't very good.

JAMES. I see.

JIM. It's better with Eleanor. Thank Christ!

KATE. I got pretty pissed off, I can tell you.

JIM. What's more to the point, thank *you*.

JAMES. I'm sure you did.

JIM. For reminding me that I *am* naturally monogamous.

KATE. There were always apologies and peace offerings but he began to take me for granted.

JIM. I love my wife, so let's go home.

KATE. So the next time he was late I made sure another fellow was there when he arrived. That soon cured him.

JAMES. When you say another fellow was *there*, d'you mean — ?

KATE. We were in bed, yes.

JIM. You're out of your depth here. Go!

KATE. I wanted to make clear I'd never be exclusively *his*. As Agnes had been. I don't believe in that.

JIM. Nor do I and yet —

JAMES. Did Albert?

KATE. Not after that, no. You didn't think we were totally loyal?

JAMES (*shrugs*). *I* am.

KATE. No!

JAMES. Tonight's the first time.

KATE. Honestly?

JIM. And the last.

KATE. I'm very flattered.

JAMES. Twenty-five years.

KATE. Staggering!

JAMES. Why? Millions like like that.

KATE. I've never thought of you as one of millions. Owning and being owned. As I said, I hate ownership.

JAMES. It hasn't been like that.

KATE. No? Then what was to stop you?

JIM. Love! Affection!

KATE. You can't have lacked opportunities.

JIM. Habit!

JAMES. Almost totally, I'd say.

JIM. Cowardice!

JAMES. Picture my life.

JIM. The fear of failure.

JAMES. My respectable working life. I walk fifteen yards through the kitchen, through the back door, across the garden to the workshop. Few excuses to go outside. Now and then I've felt the need but I've suppressed it, sublimated it —

KATE. Taken yourself in hand?

Pause. JIM *laughs, then* JAMES.

JAMES. It wasn't difficult. I've enjoyed my work, the pleasure of my craft. You could say it was as much a vocation as being an original creative artist. Conserving what we had already.

KATE. Right.

JIM. This is shit. You're a second-rater.

JAMES. To work on a Matisse or a Bonnard means I play my humble part in keeping the wolves at bay. Lighting the darkness.

JIM. She'll never swallow that? She must be bursting.

JAMES. Well, that's my life. Eleanor knows what I'm doing every hour of every day.

KATE. Till now.

JAMES *nods solemnly*.
JIM *chuckles*.

Oh, God, why's life never simple? Why another married man?

JIM. You tell me.

KATE. The last thing I want is to mess with marriages. And Eleanor of all people! Such a fantastic woman.

JAMES. By Christ, isn't she? Outspoken, tolerant, realistic. Sensual.

KATE. We're very much alike in that way.

JIM. You're not sensual. Just pretending.

JAMES. Wonderfully sane as well.

JIM. Those words you used when you were coming. That wasn't sensuality. That was to help me, wasn't it?

KATE. So unlike Agnes in every way.

JIM. Was it? To help me?

JAMES. She can't stand Agnes.

JIM. Or did I really excite you?

JAMES. All bitter and twisted.

KATE. Thanks for warning me, by the way.

JIM. Come on, man.

KATE. About Agnes.

JAMES. The Requiem's finishing. I must go, dear.

KATE. Come and stir my cup again soon.

She kisses him, as before, at length.

JIM. Far less alarming, the tongue, now it's not in public. Also she smokes too much. (*He moves towards the door, saying to* JAMES:) Come on, man, it's up to you to finish.

JAMES *ends the kiss and turns to go. She moves towards the door.*

JAMES. It might be as well if you came to dinner. Then I can give you those names I gave you at our lunch.

KATE. And I can invite you both to my Private View.

JAMES. Absolutely!

KATE. I'll ring her and fix it.

They go off.

The Fugue swells and ends or fades away. The lights go out on KATE's *room.*

JIM (*comes downstage and speaks as though to the absent* JAMES). Home well before her and no suspicion. She was so full of the concert and how badly the soloist had sung the Recordare. Entirely trusting. What with the shallow excitements of Kate, the relief at having got away with it and Eleanor's pleasure in her evening, I was moved by a fondness I hadn't felt for years.

JAMES (*re-entering with him*). So much so that I almost wished I'd spent the evening with her instead.

JIM. Almost.

JAMES. I was aching to tell her where I'd been.

JIM. We'd always said we would.

JAMES. The fact remains I didn't. As it was a solitary episode, over as soon as started, I thought it was best forgotten.

JIM. So you'd enjoyed the broadcast —

JAMES. Nobody had telephoned —

JIM. Which I knew because I'd left the answering machine turned on —

JAMES. And my love for the woman who shared my life was soon a tremendous physical desire.

JIM. That night and the next few days you were never off the nest.

JAMES. We hadn't made love like that for years.

JIM. Then Kate invited herself to dinner and both of us trod a minefield of lies all evening with Eleanor, trying to remember what she was supposed to know and not know —

JAMES has gone up into the living-room and ELEANOR opens the hall door and comes in.

ELEANOR (*calls off*): Bye-bye Kate. See you Tuesday at the gallery.

She closes the door. JAMES waits for her to return to the living-room. As she enters, he yawns.

JAMES. Quarter past twelve. A slight improvement.

ELEANOR doesn't answer but bustles about clearing up.

I've done the ashtray. Ten cigarette-ends.

JIM (*joining them in the room*). Why doesn't she answer?

JAMES. You must admit I'm right. She *is* a pale imitation of Albert.

Pause. ELEANOR collects glasses.

JIM (*urgently, to* JAMES): Has she got there? Christ.

JAMES. Well, we've done our duty for another month.

ELEANOR. Not quite.

She leaves the room for the hall, taking the glasses out. JAMES follows.

JAMES. What d'you mean?

JIM. She means Kate's invited us to her —

ELEANOR. She's invited us to her Private View. (*She goes off to the kitchen.*)

JAMES. Her Private View of what?

JIM. If she's even slightly suspicious, say you'd rather not go.

ELEANOR (*returning*). What d'you think?

JAMES. Well, photographs presumably. Isn't that what she is, a photographer?

ELEANOR. Her photos of the Far East, yes, taken when she and Albert were there together.

JAMES. Oh no!

ELEANOR. Oh, yes! She asked me in the kitchen.

JAMES. Why didn't she ask us both together?

ELEANOR. She was afraid you'd say 'Oh, no', that's why. Afraid you'd bite her head off.

JIM. She's nowhere near!

JAMES. Me?

ELEANOR. You have been all the evening.

JAMES. *I* have?

ELEANOR. Ever since Albert's death, in fact.

JAMES. I wasn't aware of it.

ELEANOR. You're not a very aware person.

JIM (*sympathetically*). Oh, my darling —

ELEANOR. — or else you'd see your good opinion means a lot to her.

He has bolted the front door. She has put out the living-room lights.

JIM (*to* JAMES): Like taking sweets from a baby.

ELEANOR. And yet when you're not biting her head off, you're yawning and looking at your watch.

JAMES. I sent her that list of names and addresses in the Middle East.

ELEANOR. She told me. But I should have thought you might have taken her out —

JIM. Taken her out?

ELEANOR. — and described all the people and how to approach them.

JAMES. Taken her out?

ELEANOR. She sees you as a sort-of irascible uncle figure who has to be appeased.

JAMES. How d'you know?

ELEANOR (*at the base of the stairs*). What?

JAMES. How d'you know she doesn't see me as a very attractive man?

JIM. Careful!

JAMES. She *said* she did.

ELEANOR. She probably does because you are. But as she can't expect any change in that department is it too much to ask you to go and see her Private View?

JAMES. Too much by far. All up to the West End to drink Algerian Burgundy while a gang of bluffers shout at me through a cloud of tobacco smoke —

They have climbed the stairs and she turns at the bedroom door, angrily.

ELEANOR. It wouldn't hurt you to do something generous for once! An act that didn't, in some way, contribute to your own selfish pleasure! (*She goes into the bedroom.*)

JAMES (*following*). All right, all right, have it your own way. We'll go. (*He slams the door behind them.*)

JIM rushes up the stairs.

JIM. Brilliant! Bravo!

A burst of joyful singing from the ode in Beethoven's Ninth.

The entire Company comes on, moving screens to reveal KATE's blown-up photographs: Japanese and Chinese faces, city scenes, temples, squalor. They are clearly guests at the Private View, drinking, smoking, talking and laughing forcibly. KATE, wearing a plain black cocktail dress, moves across exchanging words, embraces, with guests. At the entrance she greets ELEANOR and JAMES who are just arriving. JIM has moved across from the bedroom door and follows KATE; he watches as they greet one another. KATE hands them glasses of red wine from a waiter's tray.

The music ends. Now we hear the more subdued buzz of party talk.

KATE. Great to see you.

ELEANOR. We said we'd come.

KATE. Great, really.

ELEANOR. I see a few familiar faces.

JAMES. Several important critics.

KATE. Right.

ELEANOR. Are they the ones with pubic hair on their chins?

JAMES. Absolutely.

ELEANOR. That's the only way I remember.

She and JAMES *laugh.*

JIM (*to* KATE). This is not the kind of Private View I want of you. For example, I'd rather see that dress in a heap on the floor.

KATE *leads* ELEANOR *and* JAMES *to meet other guests and leaves tem talking while she meet others.* JIM *stays with her as she drifts away.*

Or hanging on a door the way it was yesterday afternoon. And you in that underwear! Are you wearing it now? And that was astounding the other night in our house, with Eleanor in the next room dealing with a music student, — forgotten already? Shall I say it then, in front of all these people? (*He turns to them all.*) She took my hand and placed it high on her thigh, raising her skirt and slightly opening her legs. She wasn't wearing anything above the stockings except the belt. And all the time we kept talking in loud voices about Cartier-Bresson and was photography an art. And sotto voce I told you how the nakedness excited me.

JAMES *is concentrating on his group but is in a good position to look across at* KATE. *She greets another man, kissing him on the mouth.*

JIM. Hullo, is he getting the tongue?

The kiss ends. JIM *shouts across to* JAMES.

No, not time enough!

No-one, of course, takes any notice.

But has he got the look of someone who's already had it?
Have *all* these men? When they talk to her, their faces get so
mawkish. (*To one of the men:*) You can't possibly think
that's attractive? That alcoholic simper?

KATE *moves to another and* JIM *follows and speaks to him.*

That superior scowl? Do I do that? How can women find men
bearable? But obviously they *do. She* does.

The man puts his arm round KATE.

How d'you find the thought they've been there? Above the
stockings? Every one of them? I welcome it. I savour it.
Reminds me how unimportant the whole thing is. Either or
both of us could finish whenever we liked and the other
wouldn't care. But then again, what *is* essential? Man can't live
by bread alone and once you've tasted honey . . .

JAMES *and* ELEANOR *move to look at the exhibits.* JIM
goes with KATE *to another group and points to* JAMES.

Look at me. I'm over here with my wife, ostensibly studying
your snaps but actually begging you to look in my direction
and speak to me with your eyes.

KATE *laughs with some guests.*

Yes, me, the well-known husband! Please!

ELEANOR *has left* JAMES, *goes to* KATE.

You looked! Our eyes met. I made you, with the force of my
lust for you.

After a word or two, ELEANOR *leads* KATE *back to*
JAMES. *They discuss one of the photographs.*

Thanks, my dear, for fetching the girl I sleep with. So that
she can promise with her eyes to be there next time I
telephone and prepare herself (*To* KATE:) like you did
yesterday — by washing away all traces of perfume, dressing

in black stockings and suspenders — (*Then to* ELEANOR:)
— yes, I know I didn't, but people *change*, that's what it's
all about — change — (*And to* KATE *again:*) — and you'll
wait on the bed you and Albert used to share while on
the radio Eleanor and a hundred other choristers sing the
Ode to Joy.

*Again the music bursts out. The exhibition disappears as
swiftly as possible by the guests turning the screens as they
go out.*

JAMES *and* JIM *come forward and down and occupy the
phone booth.* JAMES *takes coins from his pocket, sets them
on the box in a pile, dials.*

KATE *enters by the door of her room as lights go up there.
She's dressed as before, makes straight for the phone and
lifts the receiver.
The music ends.*

KATE. Yes?

The pay tone is heard till JAMES *feeds in coins.*

JAMES. James here. James Croxley. Hullo?

KATE. How are you?

JAMES. Oh, not too bad. How are things with you?

KATE. I've been pretty busy. Which is good.

JAMES. Good. That's good. When am I going to see you again?

KATE (*shrugs*). Name the day. You know my number.

JAMES. It's not that easy. Eleanor's hardly ever out. Once or
twice I rang from home while she was shopping but you
weren't there.

KATE. Most days I'm out.

JAMES. I can sometimes get away to shop for turps or framing.
Evenings are tricky. I've come for a jog on the Common but
the first three phones had been vandalised. When can I see you?

KATE. Tonight's no good.

JAMES. No, not tonight.

JIM. What's she doing tonight, I wonder?

JAMES. But how about next Monday? Eleanor's rehearsing, the first time for weeks.

KATE. Oh, bloody hell, I'm in Cornwall Monday and Tuesday, covering the St. Ives crowd. Any other evening next week — ?

JAMES. That's the only one.

JIM. First: jealousy. Then relief. Let off the hook.

KATE. I'm sorry, I really am.

JIM. No danger Monday night. You can get your breath back.

JAMES. Two weeks since your Private View.

JIM. Your heart can slow down.

KATE. I know. Too long.

JIM. You can go back to sleep again.

JAMES. There's so much I want to say to you Kate, but I can't talk on the phone, and anyway this has become a marathon jog.

KATE. Would you like to write?

JAMES. Write?

KATE. A letter, yes.

JIM. Better not. So far it's only between the two of us. A letter she could show to Eleanor —

KATE. Darling —

JIM. There'd be proof. She could tele —

JAMES. I'd better not.

JIM. After all, what do you know about her? What does *anyone* know about her?

KATE. Don't you trust me? To keep it dark?

JIM *puts a hand over his mouth.* JAMES *frowns.*

JAMES. Of course I trust you. So yes, I'll write.

JIM (*breaking away*). Dear Kate —

KATE. Of course, you won't get any answer —

JAMES. No, of course not —

JIM (*in the workshop*). Dearest Kate —

KATE. Except I could write to both of you with secret messages for you to find . . .

JIM. My darling —

KATE. Art postcards. Classical tits and bums.

JAMES. Be careful . . .

> KATE *laughs and lights go on her. She goes.* JAMES *comes to* JIM, *writing the letter.*

JIM. Darling Kate, I suddenly realised this is the first love-letter I've written for twenty-five years. So try to overlook the stilted phraseology.

JAMES. Is it a good idea to mention that? Does it make me unattractive?

JIM. I'm using muscles that haven't moved for so long they're bound to creak a bit. (*Reading the letter*:) Anyway this isn't a love-letter, is it? That's why I'm so grateful. Love's got nothing to do with it. We ask nothing of each other except the occasional hour together and the pleasure of our bodies.

> *Lights up on a tea-room, similar to the restaurant.* ELEANOR *and* AGNES *enter and take the free table. A* WAITRESS *comes to take their order.*

JAMES. I wish it could be longer though. It can't ever be as good as with Eleanor when there's so little time.

JIM. I can't imagine why a nice young girl —

JAMES. A lovely girl —

JIM. Why a fantastic girl like you should offer herself without strings to an old man —

JAMES. An older man —

JIM. — to a man like me — but who's counting?

JAMES. It's the kind of thing men want and women loathe, they always say. Then why?

JIM. Whatever the reason, thanks.

The WAITRESS *leaves the table.* ELEANOR *and* AGNES *talk.*

Because what you've brought me is not only marvellous fun but pure.

JAMES. It must be pure because I'm no catch.

AGNES. Oh, yes, I'm much better, thanks. My new work's exhausting but well worthwhile. We're really making progress towards a better deal for battered wives.

ELEANOR. High time.

AGNES. And as a battered wife myself I feel —

ELEANOR (*laughing*). Oh, come on —

AGNES. No, I mean, it's partly a sublimation for my battered feelings but that's neither here nor there as long as I do some good.

ELEANOR. Absolutely.

AGNES. All do-gooders want to do themselves a bit of good as well.

The WAITRESS *brings their tray.*

JIM. Whereas, of course, marriage is anything but pure.

JAMES. It's ownership and children and duty and illness —

JIM (*to him*): And joint accounts and property —

JAMES. And being an open book —

JIM (*reading the letter*): But I won't go into that —

JAMES. Heavy scene, man.

They laugh as ELEANOR *pours tea.*

ELEANOR. I'm so relieved you're better. Tell the truth, I felt you were dwelling morbidly on Albert's memory.

AGNES (*taking tea*). *Did* you?

ELEANOR. You were so vindictive to Kate.

AGNES. You think so?

ELEANOR. And, as there wasn't any way you could hurt her, the only sufferer had to be you.

JIM. So not to get into that whole heavy scene —

JAMES. Yes, she'll like that —

JIM — let me simply say I feel no guilt about having *you*, only a little in deceiving *her*.

AGNES. You underestimate me. We can make her suffer too.

ELEANOR. We?

AGNES. Oh, the children are with me. Some time ago, as part of a slimy attempt to win Susie over to his side, Albert gave her a key to the flat. The one where whatshername's still living. She never knew. We've been using it to get in there and inventory the contents.

ELEANOR. Oh, Agnes, no.

AGNES. Oh, Eleanor, yes. From the Oriental rugs to the Irish tea-towels.

ELEANOR *shakes her head. The* WAITRESS *brings cakes*.

ELEANOR. My dear, I'm very fond of you, I can't let you destroy your own peace of mind like this.

AGNES. Peace of mind is ignorance.

ELEANOR. You know that isn't true.

AGNES. Oh, I've learnt it is. The only real peace of mind comes from punishing evil.

ELEANOR. She's not evil, she's a good-time girl.

AGNES. A star-fucker? That's what I thought. All the same she destroyed my marriage.

ELEANOR. Agnes, don't be angry at what I'm going to say. Something must have gone wrong already. With your marriage. I mean, would he have left you five years earlier?

JIM. So few adventures in life are pure and harmless.

JAMES. This must be. There's nothing else in it for her. Pure. Unadulterated.

ELEANOR. I'm sorry that sounds unkind but if old friends can't be helpful, who can?

AGNES. What should we do without old friends?

ELEANOR. Why don't we talk about something else? It obviously upsets you —

AGNES. Oh, no, one good turn deserves another. I'd like to help *you* too.

JIM has taken an official-looking envelope and writes an address. JAMES has got out a dictionary and is looking up a word.

JAMES. Adult, adulter, adulterate, adulterer, adultress, adulterise, adulterous, adultery . . .

AGNES. When Susie was in the flat one day, the star-fucker being fucked in Sweden at the time, the mail came bumping through the front door onto the welcome mat.

JAMES. Adulterate. To render counterfeit, corrupt, by base admixture.

JIM. The opposite of pure.

He puts a stamp on the envelope. AGNES opens her bag and takes out an exactly similar envelope.

AGNES. She opened all the official-looking letters to see if there was something we should be sharing.

ELEANOR. Honestly, Agnes, reading people's mail!

JAMES. Violation of the marriage-bed. Idolatry.

AGNES. And as it turned out, there was.

JAMES. Enjoyment of a benefice during the translation of a bishop.

He and JIM laugh.

JIM. Trust the bloody clergy to get it wrong.

He scans the last part of the letter as JAMES puts away the dictionary and looks at a painting on the easel.

ELEANOR does not immediately take the letter but looks at it.

AGNES. You'll recognise the handwriting?

JAMES. Words and pictures are supposed to pin down meaning. But it's all ambiguous.

ELEANOR *takes the letter.*

What's pure is *im*pure. Adulteration can clarify.

During a pause the sounds of the tea-room swell briefly while ELEANOR *reads and* AGNES *sips her tea.* NELL *enters, dressed like* ELEANOR, *and sits between the two women.*

NELL (*reading*): 'Of course I'm longing to be in your bed again but there aren't many chances to leave the house. Later this year there's the Matthew Passion and towards Christmas Messiah and the Mozart Requiem and Messiah. Some — or all — of these I hope we shall be listening to together.'

JAMES. With half an ear.

JIM (*writing*). With — half — an — ear.

NELL. 'If I can come at a time you haven't any other callers, though I understand I have no claims on you. Any more than you on me. Which strikes me as a perfect arrangement. And sometimes when you come round here, we'll feel each other up while Eleanor's in the music-room. I liked it when you spilt wine from your mouth into mine. So — till the next rehearsal of a Passion here's thinking of you, love, all manner of kisses — '

ELEANOR *folds the letter and returns it to* AGNES.

JIM *folds it too and the two letters are returned to the envelopes together.* JIM *seals his.*

AGNES. Join the club. I've poured some tea.

ELEANOR. Thank you.

AGNES. I never meant to show you that.

NELL. No? Why bring it then?

ELEANOR. I'm glad you did.

AGNES. Glad — ?

NELL. How could he do this to me?

ELEANOR. Glad, certainly, you didn't keep it to yourself, as it obviously troubled you so much.

NELL. How could he risk humiliating me? In front of her?

ELEANOR *sips her tea.*

AGNES. Doesn't it trouble *you*?

ELEANOR. It troubles me you and Susie have read this letter. Has anyone else?

AGNES. Of course not.

NELL. My cheeks are burning.

AGNES. D'you want to keep it?

NELL. She's bound to notice.

ELEANOR. That might be best.

NELL. My world's caved in but I'm sitting here.

ELEANOR (*taking the letter*). Thanks.

NELL. Come on, get away as quick as you —

AGNES. Eleanor, love, I only wanted to put you on your guard by a couple of subtle hints — but when you started *defending* her and saying she was harmless, I knew it was time to show you the letter.

NELL. Come on, you're enjoying every minute.

ELEANOR. I didn't call her 'harmless'. I said she wasn't evil, that's all. I think the letter proves it. And, of course, I knew she fancied James. In fact I told him.

NELL. That much is true, make do with that.

AGNES. But did you know they listened to your concerts in the bed she used to share with Albert?

NELL. Try not to imagine it.

ELEANOR. He wants a bit on the side, why not?

She shrugs and smiles, drinks tea.

AGNES. That's what Albert called it too.

NELL. Make your mind a blank.

AGNES. His very words.

NELL. She pities you.

AGNES. A bit on the side. It's nothing, he said when I found out, she's nothing to me.

NELL. Think of nothing or you'll cry.

AGNES. James's letter, word for word. Be more tolerant, he used to say. More easy-going. He stood for tolerance. The permissive society. He did as much as anyone to advertise its virtues.

NELL. Why write a letter? Why take that risk?

AGNES. Well, now we see what that's led to — abortion, drugs, the kids on drink, apathy on one side and a neo-fascist law-and-order reaction on the other.

NELL. Shut up.

AGNES. It's not the first time liberalism's failed us. We should know better. Stop it now.

NELL. Shut up. I said!

AGNES. Don't try appeasement. You'll end at your own little Munich.

NELL. Come on.

JAMES *starts to use the phone.*

ELEANOR. Shan't be a minute, Agnes . . .

AGNES. Shall I come with you?

NELL. Haven't you had enough?

ELEANOR *goes, colliding with the* WAITRESS.

The dissonant fanfare from the Choral Symphony.

During this, lights fade on the tea-shop as AGNES *beckons to the* WAITRESS *who brings the bill. She pays and goes.*

At the same time, JAMES *is joined in the living-room by* JIM. *Lights up on* KATE's *room show that she is talking on the phone. She has a bottle of scent in the other hand.*

The music ends.

KATE. Well, it certainly hasn't arrived.

JAMES. I hope to God it doesn't come back here.

KATE. The last few weeks a lot of my mail's gone missing.
    Personal *and* official. Luckily my *work's* arranged by phone.

JIM. Personal? That means from men.

JAMES. God save us from the British postal service.   ·

JIM (*behind him, into the receiver*): Yes, all right, you've made
    me jealous, made me wonder who the others are —

JAMES (*cutting over*): Used to be all right as the G.P.O. but
    since they started calling it 'Communications' —

KATE (*laughing*). Right.

JAMES. It's another example of the decline of work.

JIM. I wish she wouldn't say 'Right' all the time.

JAMES. To someone like me raised on the idea that excellence
    was achieved by work, by application, these are confusing
    times.

JIM (*wagging a finger at him*). Careful, Dad, that's a heavy
    scene. Moralising.

KATE. Right. Well, am I going to see you?

JAMES. I can't today. She's expected any minute.

KATE. No, not today. I've got to go out myself.

JIM (*into the receiver again*): Or some man's coming to call on
    you —

JAMES. Next Tuesday afternoon I'm going to bid for the Arabs
    at Sotheby's post-impressionist sale. I could drop in on you
    afterwards for an hour or so —

KATE. Why don't we meet there?

JIM. You might be seen.

KATE. I'd love to see you bidding. Spending all those petro-dollars.
    Very sexy.

JAMES. Oh, it's not at all, believe me —

KATE. Then you could touch me up while I'm driving the car back here. With my hands on the wheel, I'd be at your mercy.

ELEANOR *enters by the front door with* NELL. JAMES *reacts.* JIM *runs to the door to see, signals back to* JAMES.

JIM. It's Eleanor.

JAMES. Right you are then.

KATE. And I've got some soap the same as yours at home, so that I can put on perfume this time and you can shower afterwards —

JAMES. Absolutely.

KATE. So she'll never know.

JAMES. Thank you very much.

ELEANOR *listens for a moment and now hangs her coat. When she returns it is with* NELL.

KATE. I'm not just a pretty face and a pair of tits, you know —

JAMES *puts down the phone.*

NELL. Ting. D'you think that was her?

JIM *returns to* JAMES, *who stands listening.* KATE *looks at the phone, sprays her neck and ears with scent and leaves the room as lights go.*

JIM. That was Otto instructing you to buy Bonnards —

NELL. Is this what it's been then all the time?

JAMES (*going to meet her*). Hullo, love?

NELL. Is this what it's going to be like from now on?

JAMES. How are you?

NELL. So transparent! Christ, why did I never notice?

JAMES. How was your afternoon?

JAMES *tries to kiss* ELEANOR *but she evades him and goes into the living-room.* JIM *and* NELL *go with them.*

JIM. What's this? What's up with her?

JAMES. I got on pretty well. The Douanier Rousseau's nearly

finished. I ate my sandwiches — delicious, by the way — and got to feeling rather lonely. Randy.

NELL. So rang her for a horny chat?

He goes to ELEANOR *and embraces her from behind. She pushes him off.*

And now you want me for a wank?

JIM. Something's up.

JAMES. How was Agnes?

NELL (*to him*): How would you expect?

JAMES. More easy-going? Or still hard-done-by?

NELL. Bastard!

JAMES. Still the Wronged Woman?

NELL. Bastard sod!

JIM. Don't talk too much.

ELEANOR *moves about, hiding her face from him. He shrugs.*

NELL (*to* ELEANOR): Don't let it drift. You can't.

ELEANOR. Who were you on the phone to?

JAMES. Just now, you mean?

ELEANOR. As I came in.

JAMES. Otto.

JIM. The Black Widow has told her something.

JAMES. Instructing me to buy Bonnards and Signacs at the sale on Tuesday.

NELL. You can't lie to save your life.

JAMES. The sheikhs and emirs are interested so those particular painters must have gone up a few points.

NELL (*over part of this*): Wouldn't deceive a cretin surely?

JIM (*as* ELEANOR *turns*). She's been crying.

NELL. He deceived *you*.

JAMES. Can I get you a drink?

NELL. A trusting wife must be one easier than a cretin.

JAMES. Vodka and tonic?

ELEANOR's taken the letter out and hands it to him.

ELEANOR. Returned to sender.

He takes and looks at it. She gets herself a drink.

JAMES. How d'you get this?

NELL. Does it matter?

JIM. Saint Agnes.

NELL. Not from Kate, if that's what you're thinking.

JAMES. Kate told me it hadn't arrived.

NELL. When you last went to fuck her? Or on the phone as I came in?

JAMES. She was on the phone as you came in.

JIM. Truth time. Good!

JAMES. I shouldn't have written but now it's out I'm glad. You're the only one I wanted to tell and the only one I couldn't.

ELEANOR. You wanted to tell *me*?

NELL. Tell me you were screwing a girl who's younger than our daughter?

JAMES. We always said we'd tell each other if and when —

ELEANOR. *You* did. My way was to keep it dark.

NELL. Which I did.

JIM. You must have guessed, surely. I thought you must have.

JAMES. Funny how things turn out.

ELEANOR. What?

JAMES. In the event. I've told the lies and you've been straight.

ELEANOR. You can't be serious.

NELL. Go on, tell him. Wipe that self-satisfied look off his face —

JAMES. What's that mean?

NELL. That 'I've been a naughty boy but ain't I clever' expression right off his —

ELEANOR. Nothing.

JAMES. I've lied to you and I'm sorry.

ELEANOR. How long have you been shagging Kate?

JIM (*insulted*). Shagging?

JAMES. I've been meeting her for a few weeks.

ELEANOR. A few weeks and I know already! God, you couldn't fool a cretin.

JAMES. My heart wasn't in it really.

NELL. Tell him how long you lied to *him*. How long you spared *his* feelings. Go on!

JAMES. As I said, I wanted to tell you. I'm glad you know.

NELL. I didn't want to know.

JAMES. I've always been very proud of the way we trusted each other. Played fair with each other. I totally trusted you and knew you'd have told me if any other man —

ELEANOR. No, no, that wasn't what I agreed. I said if it happened spare the other's feelings.

NELL. As I did yours.

ELEANOR. Keep it dark.

JIM. She's cracked.

JAMES. I understood the opposite. If you had had a lover, you'd have told me.

NELL. You'd have been destroyed.

ELEANOR. I certainly would not have told you. You loved me then.

JAMES. I love you now.

NELL. I've read that letter! Four times. Once at the table of the tea-shop in front of the friend who gave it to me. Twice in the lavatory, once more in the train home. You called her 'darling'.

ELEANOR *shakes her head and goes for another drink.*

JAMES. Who gave you this? Was it Agnes?

NELL. How could you humiliate me in front of her?

JIM. Who else could it be?

NELL. Don't you see that's the worst of it? The loss of dignity.

JAMES. She's an interfering bitch.

ELEANOR. She's a poor widow possessed by love.

JIM. Don't keep using that word.

JAMES. Love? She wanted to hurt you.

NELL. Who gave her the opportunity?

JIM. I must warn Kate about Agnes.

ELEANOR. I thought that at first. And for some moments I considered hurting her in return. Then I decided she wanted me for an ally in her war with Kate.

JAMES. *How* could you have hurt her?

NELL. Go on, tell him. (*To him:*) She still thinks —

ELEANOR. She still thinks Albert only had one other woman. The one you've taken over.

JAMES. I haven't taken her —

ELEANOR. Whereas I know of at least one other.

JAMES. She told me there were others, yes.

ELEANOR. This was before her.

JAMES. How d'you know?

NELL. He's hooked. Go on.

JAMES. You can't be sure.

ELEANOR. I know the only way you *can* be sure.

She sits and drinks. NELL *studies* JAMES.

NELL. Are you getting there? How long can it possibly take —

JIM. Her?

JAMES. D'you mean — ?

JIM. Christ!

JAMES. You and Albert?

NELL. Talk about the Mills of God.

ELEANOR. Yes.

JAMES. Really?

NELL. Really, yes.

JIM. You never know anyone.

JAMES. When was this?

ELEANOR. In another century.

JAMES. Where? For how long?

NELL. How does it feel? Eh?

ELEANOR. I'm not going into details now —

JIM. Oh, yes, you are, —

ELEANOR. — because it wasn't important.

NELL. Even *that's* hurt him. Don't go further. Leave it there.

ELEANOR. An episode. A shoulder to cry on. After a few drinks. You were away.

JAMES. Where did you?

ELEANOR. Here. He brought me home.

JAMES. In our bed?

ELEANOR. In this room. Once. Nothing more.

JAMES *turns away to get a drink.*

JAMES. Was it all right?

ELEANOR. I'm not going into details.

JIM *goes to* JAMES *and talks inaudibly.*

NELL. That's enough. He's had enough. Don't lose your advantage by saying it was hopeless, that you both felt ashamed of betraying James. Violating the taboo of best friend's wives or husbands. Leave it at that.

JAMES *turns back, smiling.*
They chuckle together.

JAMES. I must say, he had some sauce.

JIM. In this room, eh?

JAMES. Crafty bugger.

NELL. He's smiling. He admires him even more.

JAMES. I always thought he was as straight as a die till he went for Kate. But now it seems he poked everything in sight. Including you.

JIM. Well, can you hear me? You've had my wife, I've had your girl. Still am having her. Knock for knock. All right?

He and JAMES *chuckle together.*

NELL. Christ, the camaraderie of cock. How they literally stand together! Whereas women never trust each other.

ELEANOR. You think it's funny?

NELL. Agnes can't trust me, I can't trust Kate —

JAMES. That you had Albert? Not that funny, no.

NELL. Though of course James can't trust *you* now.

JIM (*smiling*). Tit for tat.

NELL. Perhaps his smile was only a bluff. He must feel hurt —

ELEANOR. The episode with Albert was more mess than ecstasy. A quick bang after a party with the kids half asleep upstairs and Sarah Vaughan on the hi-fi. Not important.

JAMES. Like me and Kate.

NELL. But unlike the man I nearly left you for.

ELEANOR. If it's unimportant, why write a letter?

JIM (*to* JAMES): Exactly. What the hell did you write for?

NELL (*to* JAMES): Two years I had a sort of love affair and I never wrote a letter!

JAMES. I don't know.

NELL. Yes, he was in the choir. That's how we could meet once or twice a week without your finding out.

JAMES. So many years since I wrote that sort of letter. I wanted to see if I could remember how . . .

ELEANOR. You never wrote me that sort of letter.

NELL (*to* ELEANOR): Don't tell him, though. He'd discount it because you never went to bed.

ELEANOR. If it's as unimportant as you say, you won't mind giving her up?

NELL. He'd call it romantic.

JAMES. Of course not.

JIM (*warning*): Steady!

NELL. Which, of course, it was. I had the best of both worlds — him for flattery, you for bed and breakfast.

ELEANOR. So!

JAMES. So!

NELL. So you see I'm not a stranger in this house. Very much at home, in fact.

ELEANOR. There's not going to be any in-between. Either you go with her or stay with me.

JIM (*to* JAMES): Agree to anything.

JAMES. I never intended going anywhere with her. And she wouldn't want me to.

ELEANOR. Don't be simple, James.

NELL. It was your simplicity made me stay. I couldn't see how you'd manage without me.

JAMES. She doesn't want another married scene.

ELEANOR. She was after Albert and she's after you.

JIM (*thrilled, to* JAMES): D'you think that's possible?

JAMES. Absolutely not.

NELL. You'll be telling us next this is only a bit on the —

JAMES. Eleanor, for both of us this is only a bit on the side.

ELEANOR (*howling*): No!

JAMES (*angry*). What?

ELEANOR. That's what they *all* say. That's what Albert told Agnes.

NELL. About the same girl.

JIM (*to* ELEANOR): Can't you see this is doing us good?

ELEANOR. Perhaps she's funny for old men, loves her father, hates her mother, wants to hurt all women, I don't know.

JIM. This is enlarging us!

ELEANOR. Albert at least was celebrated. A star to fuck.

JAMES. You haven't stopped using off-colour language since you came in.

JIM. Fuck and bang and shagging and love.

JAMES. Albert's marriage was on its last legs. Our is different. You're not Agnes.

JIM. So don't act like her.

JAMES. She treated Albert as property. But people aren't things.

ELEANOR. So nor is Kate. Not a bit on the side but a woman.

JIM. Both.

ELEANOR. She wants to take you away from me. I know her. I was like her once. Well, go with her if that's what you want.

NELL. And if you *did* choose to go with her, where would I be? A man of fifty's still all right but a grandmother of forty-five is nobody's —

JAMES. There's no question of leaving you.

NELL. Thank God!

Choral music, perhaps 'Quan Olim Abraham' from Mozart's Requiem or a fugue from a Passion.

KATE comes on wearing a gown and arrives downstage at the same time as JIM. *Lights change.* JIM *and* KATE *face front.*

JIM. Hullo, Kate?

KATE. Hullo.

JIM. James speaking, James Croxley.

KATE. I know who it *is*.

JIM. Eleanor's found out.

KATE. Oh, no. How?

JIM. The letter I wrote got to her instead.

KATE. Through Agnes.

JIM. Yes.

KATE. I thought as much.

JIM. Of course, I'll have to write an official letter.

KATE. Of course.

JIM. Ignore it.

KATE. Right.

> JAMES *comes downstage too.* KATE *continues speaking to* JIM, *describing how she came to suspect that* AGNES *was prying. The rest of this scene till the Act ends works like this — a fugue of voices with the written speeches predominating and improvised dialogue continuing behind.*

JAMES. Dear Kate, it doesn't matter how but Eleanor's discovered we've been meeting. I suppose it's only natural she should be upset but I've tried to explain it was only a lark and there's no question of anything more.

ELEANOR (*joining them, while* JAMES, KATE *and* JIM *continue*). Dear Kate, I haven't read his letter but I hope James didn't give the impression I'm getting melodramatic. There's no need for any of us to get into a heavy scene, as he calls it.

KATE. Dearest Eleanor, thank you so much for writing. The worst thing about all this is the pain I've caused you —

NELL (*joining them*). Oh, yes, I'm sure —

KATE. — and the thought of losing your friendship.

NELL. You do seem to have your work cut out staying friendly with the wives.

ELEANOR. I've told him he's at liberty to go with you but if he does, it's for good. No using you as lover and me as safety-net.

NELL. You have him and the best of luck. Find out for yourself what fun it is to be the wife of a man who works at home.

JAMES. Eleanor and I both hope that, when this has spent itself, we'll all three pick up the pieces again and meet as friends . . .

NELL. No chance of a break or change of scene. Well, you've given him that. So take him, do his washing, his V.A.T. . .

KATE. Let's please meet and talk as soon as I'm back from the Far East.

JIM. I know that while you're — where is it? —

KATE. Kyoto, Tokyo, Nagasaki, Los Angeles, San Francisco —

JIM. Yes, I know you'll have every man who takes your fancy —

KATE. Is it enough to say at the moment that my affection and respect for you have never diminished?

NELL. I'd rather be the mistress, with all the little mistressy excitements: will he come today, will *she* find out? I might suggest that — let him live with you and sneak away whenever he can for a crafty fuck with me.

JIM. And, though I long to be in their place, I don't resent you having those men. We don't love each other and you don't love them —

NELL. And I'll dress in frilly undies and wear exotic scent and enjoy the aphrodisiac of fooling you, the wife.

JAMES. And if by any chance Susie or Agnes is reading this, do let it through because it's written with Eleanor's approval and I've kept a carbon copy. (*To* ELEANOR:) Let's go for a lie-down, shall we?

ELEANOR. Why not? Two hours before my student comes.

JIM. All I ask is, while you're having them, spare a thought for me. On similar occasions I'll remember you . . .

JAMES *and* ELEANOR *move to the stairs.*

KATE. I'm so brought down and confused by all the trouble I've caused . . .

JIM. By Christ, Kate, I'll miss you . . .

KATE. . . . you'll survive . . .

JIM. Just about . . .

KATE. Till I get back . . .

JAMES and ELEANOR have climbed the stairs and near the top JAMES begins caressing her. She responds and they embrace on the top step.

NELL. Listen to his fifty-year old moans about his failing health health . . . his wasted life, the girls he never had , , ,

JIM. Send a sexy card —

KATE. All right —

JIM. With a hidden message for me —

NELL. But why should you take him from me? He's mine! I love him!

They all continue.
JAMES and ELEANOR make love on the landing.
Music drowns all voices.

Act Two

The Chorale 'O Haupt voll Blut und Wunden' from Bach's St Matthew Passion is heard.

ELEANOR and NELL are in the living-room by evening light. ELEANOR has a long drink and is on the sofa marking her score of Matthew Passion but also listening to NELL, who walks about reading a letter.

NELL. 'Dear James, it's funny writing a letter to someone you live with, but there are things to say *now* that I suddenly find I can't say to your face.'

She breaks off as ELEANOR drains her glass and goes for another drink.

'We've both of us avoided mentioning Kate during the last few weeks while she's been away but now I wish she'd come home. I certainly don't hate her. In fact, I rather miss her. What I hated was having to be the Wronged Woman and say all the things a Wronged Woman's supposed to say. No, if anything, I'm grateful to her — '

ELEANOR (*returning with drink*): How can I say that? Grateful?

NELL. 'For bringing the colour back to our cheeks. Giving our marriage a shot in the arm. Showing we can't just drift away into the sunset doing what we've always done.'

ELEANOR. It seemed very good to me.

NELL. But not to James. He's been more alive lately, you sensed it, you told him so.

ELEANOR (*returns to sit*). And that's what I'm grateful for? Bringing my husband back to life?

NELL. Yes. Profit from that. Make it work for you.

ELEANOR. How?

The kitchen door opens and JAMES *comes in.* NELL *hides the letter.* JAMES *brings an unframed canvas.* JIM *follows, reading a book.* JAMES *puts down the painting so that we see the face of Christ. Chorus of Bach ends: 'So Schändlich Zugericht'.*

JAMES. What does all that mean?

ELEANOR. Hullo.

JAMES. What's it all about?

ELEANOR. Something like 'head full of blood and wounds, full of sorrow and scoffing, mocked with a crown of thorns'.

JAMES. I thought so. Want a drink?

ELEANOR. Got one, thank you. I'm sitting here getting quietly sloshed marking my score of the Matthew Passion. Finished the painting?

JAMES. I couldn't face any more without a glass of wine. I'd had enough of that insipid eunuch.

She looks at the picture while JAMES *gets a drink.* JIM *reads from the book.*

JIM. 'Thou hast conquered, O Pale Galilean, the world has grown grey from thy breath,
We have drunken of things Lethean, we have fed on the fullness of death . . .' Algernon Charles Swinburne . . .

ELEANOR. Has Pale Galilean been getting you down?

JAMES. Well, look at him. The self-pity. Sickly, sentimental.

ELEANOR. You're getting a lot of money, though, aren't you?

JAMES. I asked more than I thought they'd pay. And they accepted. But it's still not enough.

ELEANOR (*giggles*): Thirty pieces of silver?

JAMES *stares at her.*

JIM. She thinks it's funny. She doesn't know what you're saying. (*To her:*) This is all about *us,* what's happened to *us.* What's been happening for centuries.

JAMES. We still live in the shadow of his death. And his birth for that matter. A virgin birth. A conception and a birth without carnal love. It flies in the face of all we know and people like us don't believe it any more. But two thousand years isn't easy to forget.

ELEANOR. I like the music.

JAMES. Of course. It's Bach. But what if it's this? Sickly Victoriana?

JIM. The Holy Oil that kept the wheels turning.

JAMES. Propaganda for the satanic mills. Putting a love of God in place of love for people.

JIM. Poor old Swinburne must have had a bellyful. No wonder he spent his last years being flogged by prostitutes.

JAMES. So that even a healthy sexual passion is twisted into a craving for the infinite. The anti-lifers, the troubadours, the saints and martyrs. Saint Teresa caught by Bernini mid-orgasm, pierced by the lance of God. Anyone who's ever watched a partner in the act can see that's a statue of a woman coming.

JIM *goes, shows* ELEANOR *the book.*

NELL. He's worked himself into a lather, hasn't he?

ELEANOR. Have you been reading a book or what?

JIM (*resentfully*): Books are to help us understand.

JAMES. I do want to make some sense of my life, don't you?

ELEANOR. Of course.

JAMES. And not in terms of death.

NELL. He means her.

ELEANOR. Well, *we* don't see it like that, do we?

NELL. He means why can't he have her too?

ELEANOR. We're not Christians. I'm an atheist but I love church music and oratorio and hymns and Christmas carols. Hundreds of people singing together is the nearest we may ever come to heaven on earth. Communion.

JAMES. The Communion, the eucharist, is a ceremony based on the pre-Christian orgy.

JIM. Dearest Kate, are you doing it now? At this moment are you saying 'it's so good, darling, it's so good'!?

JAMES. The pagan fertility festivals? The Christians took them over.

ELEANOR. I meant 'communion' in the sense of people congregating.

JIM. Are you saying 'don't stop now, please' to some lucky Yank?

JAMES. People used to congregate to make love. Before the god-lovers and life-haters set down the couple as the largest legitimate sexual group.

ELEANOR. You've got sex in the head.

JIM. Where else can I have it?

NELL. She's in there, isn't she? In your head? With her frilly knickers and tricks with the wine?

ELEANOR. Has all this come from having a bit on the side?

JAMES. If it's either/or that's not the answer. If it finishes with a new monogamy.

ELEANOR. It's hard to see an alternative.

JAMES. More than one.

ELEANOR. At a time.

JIM *and* NELL *listen.*

JAMES. Why not?

ELEANOR. It's hard enough to find one person you fancy, leave alone two.

NELL. It took you twenty-five years to find *her* . . .

ELEANOR. I mean, I'm game. But where do we look?

NELL. And *she's* in California so —

ELEANOR. Shall we go through the phone-book or what?

JIM. You'd better take this seriously.

JAMES (*laughing*): We could go round the pub, see who we run into.

NELL. Anyone fancy a fertility festival?

JAMES and ELEANOR embrace.

Good clean house. Cold buffet to follow. (*She closes her eyes.*) Oh, my love, stop doing that with your tongue.

The doorbell rings.

ELEANOR. That's my student. She wants me to run through her adjudication pieces. Sorry.

JAMES. Oh well. I'd better get back to Old Killjoy here.

ELEANOR. I'm sorry.

JAMES. I'd better get back to Old Killjoy out there.

ELEANOR goes towards the door. JAMES takes the picture to the kitchen. JIM talks after ELEANOR. NELL tears up the letter and throws it away.

JIM. I won't allow my life to close in again. I got my chance and opened the door. If I can change, then so can you —

ELEANOR opens the door to KATE.

KATE. Hullo.

JIM. It's her. She's here!

ELEANOR. Good God!

KATE. Bad time?

ELEANOR. Not at all. Come in.

KATE does. ELEANOR shuts the door. JIM runs back to JAMES.

JIM. I made you come by thinking of you. By dwelling on your memory. Night and day.

KATE. You said to drop in if I was passing.

ELEANOR. Of course. Delighted.

NELL. Where would you be passing to?

ELEANOR. I thought you were still abroad?

KATE. Been back a few days.

ELEANOR *takes* KATE's *outdoor coat and goes to hang it.*
When she returns it is with NELL. KATE's *more provocatively*
dressed than usual.

JIM. A few days? Why d'you leave it a few days?

ELEANOR. You're looking well. A lovely colour.

KATE. That's California.

NELL. And dressed to kill. Kill *what*?

KATE. Won't last long in London.

NELL. Cost the earth, that little number.

ELEANOR. James is here.

NELL. The same perfume I smelt on James that day. That he
said was from expensive tarts and now I know what he meant.

They go into the living-room.

ELEANOR. We've got company.

JAMES (*turning, coming to greet* KATE). So I heard.

JIM. Kiss? No.

KATE *and* JAMES *shake hands.*

KATE. Oh, very formal. Surely we're allowed a friendly kiss?

They do, a social peck.

NELL. What's the game now? Can't be after him or she wouldn't
have come here. Or would she?

ELEANOR. Lovely tan, hasn't she, James?

JAMES. Absolutely. As you told us in your card from — where
was it?

KATE. Santa Monica?

JIM. Saucy as ever. A nude by Ingres —

KATE. You got that then?

JIM — with an arse like a peach —

JAMES. Yes, indeed.

JIM. And a hope that both of us would see your tan before it
faded away.

KATE. I'm brown all over.

JIM. Or as you said 'the tail-end of my tan'.

KATE. For the first time ever.

JIM. Tail-end!

JAMES. Can I get you a drink?

KATE. I thought you'd never ask.

JAMES. Gin and tonic?

KATE. Right.

NELL (*to* ELEANOR): Strange to watch the two of you together. First time since I found out . . .

JAMES. And you, love? Same again?

ELEANOR. Mmm?

JAMES. Same again?

ELEANOR. Please.

NELL. Aren't you drinking rather a lot?

ELEANOR. I'm not driving.

JAMES. What?

JIM. What's she talking about?

NELL. You're pissed.

She moves off unsteadily.

JIM (*to* KATE): Find a way of saying if you got my letter.

JAMES. You had a good time then?

KATE. Great, fantastic! In California anyway.

JIM. No, wait till the student comes.

ELEANOR. Get any work done?

KATE. In Japan I worked. In the States I played.

JIM. Then when Eleanor's in the music-room you can say if it's yes to Zurich.

ELEANOR. Lucky girl.

NELL. Everything's instant, isn't it? Casual. Spur of the moment.

JIM. You'll like it. Three days. Nice hotel. The lake, the mountains.

KATE. Lucky . . . in some ways.

NELL. Arrivals, departures, eating, drinking, who you sleep with.

ELEANOR. Some ways?

JIM. And while I'm working you can shop. I'm being paid in francs.

NELL. She even makes her pictures with a shutter. Instantly.

ELEANOR. Why some ways? No strings and no connections.

JAMES *has given them drinks.*

JAMES. Cheers then.

KATE. Right.

NELL. I was like you once. At art college. The free-wheeling dolly.

JIM. I'd hoped you'd reply to my dealer — marking the envelope 'to be collected'?

KATE. So here we are again, all three of us. I've missed you both. I meant what I said in my letter. This thing James and I have had, we won't let that affect our relationship, will we?

ELEANOR. We're adult people.

NELL. What's she doing here dressed to kill? What's her game?

KATE *takes* ELEANOR's *hand.*

KATE. If I'd been you I'd have scratched my eyes out.

ELEANOR. Really? No.

KATE. Yes, a very heavy scene. But it was only a lark. Wasn't it James?

JIM. I want you.

JAMES. I hope I've made that clear.

ELEANOR. He's tried.

KATE (*to* ELEANOR): I'd have felt far worse to lose *you*.

She kisses ELEANOR's *hand, then her lips.*

NELL. Is she Lesbian then?

JIM. This is either an elaborate cover or —

NELL. It would account for the string of married men.

ELEANOR. I felt the same about you.

NELL. Indirectly getting at the wives.

KATE. You may not believe this but I can't stand all that underhand business.

JIM. This is good but where's it leading?

KATE. I know you agree with me, Eleanor, that sex is terrific fun as long as it doesn't lose you friends. It should be open. Cards on the table.

JIM *and* NELL *talk to* JAMES *and* ELEANOR, *but we don't hear clearly and* KATE *continues.*

If I like the look of a man or another woman — or both — I ought to say so and see what happens. I mean, I shouldn't be put down by conventional values and start a lot of lying that nearly led to losing *both.*

She reaches for JAMES's *hand and he approaches. She holds both.*

I'm putting this very badly —

JIM. I wouldn't say that.

NELL. Oh, I don't know —

KATE. — but you know what I mean, James?

JAMES. Yes, I believe so.

JIM. Just taking your hand has given me a hard-on.

NELL. She wants us both.

KATE. I know Eleanor does. I don't mean I wasn't attracted to you, James, of course I was, but not you only. It was both of you. Your life. Your whole relationship. You know?

She kisses him, as before.

JIM. You're doing beautifully.

NELL. I can feel his desire through her. I suppose that's how it works. A sort-of conductor.

JAMES moves away. KATE breaks from ELEANOR, who sits.

ELEANOR. I'm sure he understands. I do.

JAMES. We were talking about this when you came.

JIM (*behind her*). We know what you mean, both of us.

He runs his hands up and down her body, caressing her.

KATE. Well. I realised how I felt about you both when it all came out and it was in that mood I left for Japan. I tried to keep my head by working hard while I was there but on my last night I was taking some pictures of an American diplomat and his Japanese wife who finally made it clear they'd like me to stay the night.

ELEANOR. And did you?

JIM runs his hand up her leg, kneeling now beside her. He raises her skirt, showing her thigh.

KATE. I did, yes.

JIM. Wear these clothes when you come to bed. Let Eleanor take them off.

JAMES. Japanese women seem too − I don't know − too much like porcelain − for a night of hanky-panky.

KATE. It's when the porcelain cracks, though.

NELL. The thought of another woman's never roused me but a man as well −

ELEANOR. You enjoyed it then?

NELL. *That* man −

KATE. No.

She goes to sit, leaving JIM. But he follows and kneels by her, caressing her leg. NELL goes to JAMES and embraces him.

JAMES. Why not?

NELL. Maybe this is the best solution. I'm fond of her and you desire her and I love you —

KATE. The man was only interested in stimulating *her*. I felt left out in the end. Aroused but unsatisfied.

NELL. But can I watch you have her?

ELEANOR. Perhaps somebody's always left out.

JIM. You won't be left out. I want both of you.

JAMES. But there was nothing wrong in principle?

KATE. Oh, no.

JAMES. Especially in a non-Christian country. Before the Holy Ghost started haunting us, sex in crowds was the norm. Romantic passion for one beloved was to the Greeks and Romans an affliction you hoped wouldn't happen in your family.

KATE. I must say I've usually enjoyed it, Christian country or not. Another drink, James, please.

JAMES. And you, love?

ELEANOR. A little Dutch courage, yes.

JAMES *gets the drinks.*

NELL. Who begins and how?

KATE. Anyway. I left before either of them were up and hitched back into town, which was another unsatisfactory episode —

NELL. Are you making this up?

KATE. I had to pay my fare, so to speak, while we were crawling in the traffic —

JIM. She's anyone's.

KATE. Amusing with all the other drivers peering through the smog at me, on this fellow's lap but not very satisfying.

NELL. In a moving car. It can't have been!

KATE. — so you can imagine that when I was finally sitting in the window-seat waiting for the airplane to start for the

States I was ready for anything.

JAMES (*giving her a drink*). There you are.

KATE (*tasting*). This is almost neat gin.

JAMES. We all need a stiff one.

NELL. You flatter yourself.

They laugh at his unintended joke.

JIM. At this moment I'm the luckiest man in the history of civilisation. In a room with the two women I desire most in the world —

KATE. And now, at last, I've come to the point —

JIM. — and both of them desire me and there's nothing in art or science or religion to compare with this —

KATE. Well, to cut a long story short, I've fallen head-over-heels in love.

Pause.

JAMES. Well, well —

JIM. No, Kate, don't say that, please —

ELEANOR. How nice for you!

NELL. And even nicer for me!

KATE. Right.

JIM. And don't keep saying 'right'.

KATE. Suddenly there was this beautiful guy asking if he could move my gear from the seat next to mine —

NELL. Poor James!

She approaches him as he stands smiling and sipping his drink.

KATE. Then I realised bells were ringing.

JAMES. Was it a bomb-scare?

KATE. What?

JAMES. Hi-jackers?

ELEANOR *laughs.*

KATE. No, in my head. Or wherever they ring.

JAMES. I was going to say 'Bells on a jumbo!'.

KATE. My heart was jumping. I could hardly speak. I thought to myself 'My God, it's love'.

JIM. You told me you didn't *want* love.

JAMES. I thought they always put on soothing strings.

NELL. I must say I'm relieved. But what's she doing *here*?

ELEANOR. That must be wonderful.

KATE. Yes, it is, but sad to say they were also warning-bells.

JIM. You didn't want another heavy scene.

NELL. Warning-bells?

KATE. They were saying 'go no further'. But I didn't read them then, I'm glad to say. For two weeks it was knock-out.

JIM. *We* could be knock-out.

KATE. L.A., Vegas, San Francisco . . .

JIM. I've had no chance. The odd hour —

ELEANOR. Then why the warning-bells?

JIM. But in Zurich —

KATE (*shrugs*). Oh, problems, problems —

NELL. Aaah.

JIM. Three days and nights —

JAMES. What problems exactly?

KATE. None on my side.

NELL (*to* ELEANOR): Another married man.

ELEANOR. American?

KATE. English. Lives not far from here. I'm on my way to see him now and thought, as it sort-of concerns us all, I'd break my journey to let you know. I told him 'Let's take off, I'm yours'.

JIM. Be his, by all means, but mine as well.

ELEANOR. But he's not free?

KATE. He's got commitments.

ELEANOR. About your age?

KATE. No. Fortyish.

NELL. I thought so.

KATE. Forty-fivish.

ELEANOR. And is he married?

KATE. Separated.

JAMES. Then what's the problem?

KATE. About to separate.

NELL. You mean you want to wreck his marriage?

KATE. Is that the end of the inquisition?

ELEANOR. Sorry. I was only asking.

KATE *moves about, puts her glass on the drinks shelf. The others wait.*

KATE. I didn't *choose* this to happen. I just fell in love.

JAMES. I never thought you were that romantic.

KATE. Eleanor doesn't think so either. She's cast me as a home-wrecker.

NELL. You can't stand disapproval, can you?

ELEANOR. *I* haven't cast you.

NELL. You want even the wives to love you.

KATE. You and Agnes.

JIM. Don't compare my wife with Agnes.

ELEANOR. I'm not tolerant the way she was.

JAMES. You're tolerant in different ways.

ELEANOR. I told James he could go with you or stay with me.

JAMES. And put like that I obviously stayed.

KATE. It was only a bit of fun. Now finished.

JIM (*going on his knees*). Please, Kate . . .

KATE. And we're the best of friends again.

> *She takes* ELEANOR's *hand and reaches for* JAMES's. *He takes hers. She impulsively kisses* ELEANOR.

> Aren't we?

> *She kisses* JAMES *on the cheek.*

JIM (*getting to his feet*). Insulting bitch.

NELL. She's enjoying this.

ELEANOR. You look very happy.

KATE (*shrugs*). I suppose that's being in love.

ELEANOR. I can just remember.

JAMES. I wouldn't know.

ELEANOR. He says he's never been in love.

KATE. You love each other.

ELEANOR. Oh, yes, but that's like — our daily bread. Being in love is different.

KATE. It's being alive after death.

JIM. Well, thanks.

NELL (*sympathetically*): Oh, James, she's never worth it.

ELEANOR. James won't fall in love. He's got too much self-esteem.

KATE (*pitying*). Ah . . .

> *She again kisses him on the cheek.*

JIM. If you peck me again like that, I'll bite a piece from your ear.

> *The doorbell rings.*

ELEANOR. There's my student. Why don't you keep James company for a bit?

NELL (*to her*): Don't rub salt in the wound.

KATE. I should really go.

JAMES. One for the road?

KATE. No, really, I mustn't keep him waiting.

ELEANOR goes to the front door. KATE finishes her drink.
NELL stays half-way between the hall and the room.

JIM. She's only punctual when it's new.

JAMES. Remember our first time — in the restaurant?

JIM. When you wanted me?

JAMES. You were punctual then.

KATE (*with a smile and a shrug*). Right.

JAMES. D'you know you use that word too often?

ELEANOR opens the door to admit a young woman, takes
her outer clothes and hangs them.

KATE. Which word?

JAMES. Right.

KATE. I do?

JAMES. Absolutely.

KATE. Same with you and 'absolutely'.

She goes to the hall. JAMES and JIM follow.

The WOMAN STUDENT's gone into the music room. She
starts limbering up her voice with scales.
KATE meets and kisses ELEANOR.

KATE. We must fix to go shopping.

ELEANOR. Yes, let's.

KATE. I'm sorry for any pain I caused you.

ELEANOR. All over now. Forgotten.

They embrace.

NELL. Should I be grateful? I don't know. He looks like death.

JIM. Love another man by all means but that doesn't mean I'm
suddenly repulsive. How about my letter? Zurich?

KATE. I'll ring you.

ELEANOR. Do.

She goes to the music room and almost at once the piano begins to assist the STUDENT in her scales.

JAMES. Did you have a coat?

KATE. Yes.

JAMES (*getting it*). There's quite a chill in the air tonight. *Winter* coming.

NELL. Poor James fell for your sex act. I almost did myself tonight.

JIM. My life's ending as abruptly as it began — how many weeks ago?

JAMES (*helping her on with the coat*). Here we are.

NELL. But, of course, you're really a romantic. Promiscuous people always are. I mustn't forget that glimpse of you at Albert's funeral party, leaning over a baby one of the guests had brought. So absorbed you didn't see me.

JIM. Kate, please . . .

He kisses her neck, goes on his knees before her.

JAMES. Did you get my letter?

KATE. It was nice of you to ask but, well, you see how things are.

JIM. No, I don't.

JAMES. Absolutely.

NELL. Agnes only saw the sex act, the purple dress and the hair-do, but I saw you touching the baby's fingers.

KATE. We'll see each other soon. At private views.

JAMES. Why did you do it like this?

KATE. This was the best way. (*She kisses him quickly and goes by the front door.*) Bye, James.

JAMES. Goodbye.

JIM (*following her, shouting*): I didn't know you wanted love, I'll say I love you. I'll do anything!

JAMES *closes the front door.*
NELL *goes to join* ELEANOR *in the music room.*

Chorus: 'He trusted in God'.

Lights on upper level.

Private view begins, exactly as in Act One, but now the photographs are of sexual acrobatics.

JAMES *goes up the stairs and reveals a closer view of the coupling. Guests loudly approve, clap, whistle, etc. He reveals another, the face of Bernini's Saint Teresa. Laughter and ribald comments. He gestures for the guests to follow him and leads them downstairs. They make themselves at home in the living-room while* JAMES *fetches the Christ painting. At the same time,* ELEANOR *comes from the bedroom in a nightgown and wanders along the balcony, looking over at the guests, trying not to be seen.*

JAMES *puts up the Christ and the reaction is as though this were the most obscene picture of all. Among the crowd we now distinguish* KATE, AGNES *and a* MAN *who might be Albert. He caresses them in turn.*

As ELEANOR *sees this,* JAMES *notices her and points her out to the crowd. She cowers but he calls her down and she hesitantly descends. He introduces her and they all applaud.*

ELEANOR *now takes over the lecture as* JAMES *goes into the crowd of onlookers, now waiting for* ELEANOR *to begin. But she's only concerned with* JAMES *and tries to see who he's with.*

There is a YOUNG WOMAN *behind the crowd and he stands behind her, caressing her breasts, kissing her hair and neck as she faces* ELEANOR, *listening.*

KATE, AGNES *and the* ALBERT MAN *begin catcalling for* ELEANOR *to start. This is taken up by others. Someone takes a flash photo, another plucks at the skirt of her nightdress to lift it. She covers herself and tries to move towards* JAMES *and the* GIRL *but they won't let her and*

*KATE and AGNES both embrace her, kiss her, restrain her.
JAMES has got some of the girl's clothing off and is pulling
her down onto the floor.*

*The crowd gather to watch this and surround them. ELEANOR
at last gets free and reaches this circle, pulling them away,
fighting through. She reveals JIM with the half-dressed girl,
kissing her body. Flash of camera.*

*He is amused by ELEANOR's appearance and points at her
nightdress. The GIRL is hidden by the crowd. They all go
through the various doors. JIM is the last to go.*

*The pictures upstairs go as they came, JAMES comes from
the bedroom in pyjamas and dressing-gown. Chorus ends and
lights change.*

ELEANOR is in the living-room, JAMES coming downstairs.

ELEANOR. Then suddenly it was in this room, and I was up
there trying to hide and you called me down in my nightdress to talk about the Christ painting —

JAMES. It was a nightmare. We all have nightmares. We don't
have to spend the rest of the night going over —

ELEANOR. Meanwhile — at the back of the crowd you were
taking off her clothes.

JAMES. Whose clothes? Kate's?

ELEANOR. No, it's not Kate. I know that. Someone else.

JAMES. Listen, will you believe me? There isn't anyone else.
There never has been anyone else but her.

ELEANOR. How can I believe you? Ever again?

JAMES. Are you trying?

ELEANOR. You *lied* to me. You broke our trust.

JAMES. You lied to *me*! Over Albert.

ELEANOR does not speak.

By your own admission. How do I know that was the only
time?

She still doesn't speak.

What is it?

ELEANOR. What?

JAMES. You seemed to be listening to something.

ELEANOR. Albert was nothing, I told you. I didn't change because of that. You didn't even notice.

JAMES. *I* haven't changed. Shall I make you some tea?

ELEANOR. Just get me a glass of Perrier.

He goes to the kitchen.

Not changed, no. Become hidden. I hardly recognise you any more. Abstracted, irritable. All you want to do is sleep. You lie there snoring and when at last I drift off I dream I'm singing an aria in the wrong key while you and Albert and Kate and Agnes sit in the front row —

JIM *returns from the kitchen with water, dressed as* JAMES *was.*

JIM. Of course all I want to do is sleep when every night is spent picking over the same old entrails —

ELEANOR. You nod off over a book, in front of the TV, during concerts —

JIM (*over*): — Looking for the same bad omens —

ELEANOR. — sleep is your way of getting through. Or is she so demanding you can't even keep awake?

JIM. Who? Who's 'she'? Kate?

ELEANOR. Not Kate, no. I know that's over —

JIM. There's no-one else.

ELEANOR. Then why does so much of your work these days take you away from home?

JIM. So much?

ELEANOR. Two days a week at least.

JIM. Most men are away for five —

ELEANOR. You're not most men.

JIM. All right. I feel the need to get away. Nowadays, if there's a choice, I work at a gallery instead of here, yes —

ELEANOR. And when I ring you aren't there.

JIM. *Once* I wasn't there. I was running in the park. You won't even allow my jog on the common any more.

ELEANOR. I'm frightened alone.

She is crying. He embraces and holds her.

You never used to go away. We spent most of our lives together.

JIM. I've tried to persuade you that was wrong.

ELEANOR. You never wanted to go outside *then*.

JIM. How d'you know?

ELEANOR. You never *said*.

JIM. I should have done. Variety is an aphrodisiac. Our married friends spend whole days apart. Without accounting. People need that freedom and privacy —

ELEANOR. *I* don't. You *didn't*.

JIM. Well, you were an untiring wife and mother. I worked hard to keep the family. Where many of our friends chanced their arms, took selfish risks with their children's futures, blew the lot on weekends away and sometimes tried a change of partner —

ELEANOR (*over this*): You didn't *want* that — ˑ

JIM (*not pausing*): — you and I made the long sure haul with no surprises. And one day we looked around to find our children gone. And you particularly were at the stage of life when every woman undergoes an inevitable change —

ELEANOR (*breaking away*). Oh, no!

JIM (*angrily*): What?

ELEANOR. Not the change of life?

JIM. Whether you like the fact or not, my dear, you've reached the age when women suddenly —

ELEANOR. Go mad. Yes?

JIM. Can't feel the ground beneath their feet.

ELEANOR *shakes her head.*

ELEANOR. They go mad. *I'm* going mad. I feel it. What shall I do?

JIM. It isn't madness, love. It's an unwillingness to change.

ELEANOR. You keep on about change. But into what? A princess? A frog?

JIM. First you accept the need to. Then you find out. It's a question of bend or break at times. (*He leads her towards the stairs.*) Not only individuals but whole nations. Families are little countries. If they can't change they die. That last time Kate was here, for instance, you and I had accepted the thought of a sexual trio.

ELEANOR. It's always this. When you say 'change' you mean I must get used to the thought of —

JIM. Will you allow me to finish?

ELEANOR. Not if all you have to say is —

JIM. I am trying to help you.

ELEANOR. Then tell me what to do!

JIM. I hesitate to suggest this but I'm desperate —

ELEANOR. You're desperate?

JIM. I think we should get some outside help.

ELEANOR. Doctors?

JIM. I don't like it either but —

ELEANOR. Both of us.

JIM. Both of us, right. But first of all, you. Would you like me to arrange a check-up with Michael at the Middlesex? A physical first and if that's all right and you're still depressed, I dare say he'll be able to put you onto some other department.

ELEANOR. Us. Not me.

JIM (*gently*): It's you that's having the nightmares.

ELEANOR. It's you that brought them on.

JIM. The doctors may not agree. In fact, it may be best if you
    don't mention that business with Kate at all . . . They'd seize
    on that.

*They've reached the upper landing now and go into the
bedroom.*

A slow chorus from the St Matthew Passion.

A DOCTOR *enters, leading* NELL. *He speaks to her kindly,
offers a chair on which she sits. He sits near her, opens a
notebook, asks a question, she shakes her head, answers. We
hear none of this, until the music ends.*

NELL. No, it started only recently. As long as we had one
    daughter left at home, I felt useful but James had begun to
    think he'd given up too much of his life to the family. When
    the last went away to training college, it seemed to mark the
    beginning of freedom for the two of us. So I looked around
    for him but found he was occupied elsewhere. Out to lunch.
    No-one home. I saw there was no-one home at all, except
    me. And half the time I was out to lunch myself. Dozing
    through a Passion. One day in rehearsal I found myself in
    tears when we sang 'Deliver me from the lion's mouth, call to
    me lest the bottomless pit shall swallow me . . .' Not tears for
    the dead or mankind in general but for myself . . . I'd sung
    them for years without thinking and now I realised that behind
    the noble Latin noise there was a meaning for me . . . my day
    of wrath was coming . . .

Music again. The DOCTOR *moves across behind her, reading
the note he's made. She turns to listen to him and, as he
stands centre, lights come up slightly on the living-room and*
JIM *comes in with the* GIRL *from* ELEANOR's *nightmare.
By the front door. She looks around as though she's never
seen the house before.*

It isn't fair to James, he spends hours of every day alone
with a painting . . . when he comes back into the world he

wants a sexy girl-friend, not a mental case, a woman whose true
self is screaming with despair . . .

The DOCTOR *has listened, now crosses to the side, making a
note.* NELL *keeps her eyes on the living-room, where* JIM *leads
the* GIRL *to the stairs, caressing her as they climb.*

. . . if this is the change of life, I'd like some pills to regulate
the chemistry . . . or at least to stop these dreams . . .

JIM *and the* GIRL *continue along the balcony into the
bedroom.*
The DOCTOR *nods, writes and gives* NELL *a prescription.*
Music resumes. The DOCTOR *asks her another question.*

. . . not always in the same place, no. But always the same
girl. A junior partner in this gallery . . . he finds any excuse to
go there . . . I think he sometimes has her in our house . . . he
leaves the windows open but enough of the scent still hangs
about . . .

ELEANOR *comes from the side to join her.*

ELEANOR (*to* NELL): You sure you're not remembering you
and Albert? You haven't confessed to that, have you? You
told James but you haven't told the doctor about him — or
Richard for that —

NELL (*as though answering the* DOCTOR): No, it's not Kate. I
know that's over. She told us both she'd fallen for another
man, so my husband had no choice.

ELEANOR. If he had, d'you think he'd have given her up for
you?

NELL. She and I are friends again. We go shopping together . . .

ELEANOR. As you gave up Richard for him?

NELL. No, it certainly isn't her. Perhaps it isn't anyone.

ELEANOR. You know he's up to something, he's so remote . . .

NELL. He's always been a distant person. He was an only child,
his parents spoilt him. They brought him up to believe in a life
based on: take and it shall be given unto you.

ELEANOR. You promised James you wouldn't tell this man all the secrets of your marriage.

NELL. So he finds love a mystery.

ELEANOR. And not only have you done that, you're running him down.

NELL. He admits that himself. He doesn't know what the words mean. He says: why call affection, lust, belief in God, patriotism, care for children, etcetera, by one word?

ELEANOR. Fostering's one thing, fucking's another.

NELL. We all recognise red, orange, yellow, blue, green and violet but we don't call them white just because they all become that when they're mixed together. He's trained himself to be precise about colours. Other people don't really see . . .

Music. Lights change. NELL gets up and moves to the clothes cupboard by the front door. She takes out a coat. JAMES comes from the kitchen, doesn't see NELL, looks at his watch, looks upwards at the balcony as though guessing where she is. ELEANOR sits in the chair near the DOCTOR. She turns to the DOCTOR and speaks silently. JAMES moves towards NELL, sees her. Music ends.

JAMES. Ah. You off now?

NELL. Yes.

JAMES. So am I. For a walk on the common. I did tell you. Possbly half an hour but it could be longer.

NELL. I didn't ask how long you'd be.

JAMES. If I undertake to be back within forty-five minutes, would that be acceptable?

NELL. Take as long as you like. I'll be out the whole afternoon, as you know. At the doctor's.

JAMES (*putting on a coat*). Tearing me apart?

NELL. He doesn't tear you apart.

ELEANOR (*to the* DOCTOR): He resents it if I say we've talked about him.

JAMES (*shrugs*). He says I'm treating you badly.

NELL looks in a glass, repairs her make-up, sits to do so. JAMES, behind her, looks at his watch.

ELEANOR. Doesn't like me seeing you at all, in fact.

NELL. He's only trying to help.

JAMES. By moralising about my behaviour? I thought shrinks weren't meant to allocate blame.

NELL. He's not a shrink. He's a clinical psychiatrist.

ELEANOR. It smacks of the church, he says, employing a professional to listen to our secrets. It means we've lost faith in human intercourse. Doctors for when the body fails, yes, or the chemistry's unbalanced but human questions need human answers.

JAMES. Well, I hope everything goes well. Hope he can be some help.

He moves towards the front door.

NELL. Are you walking across the common towards the station? Let's stroll across together.

JAMES. I'm going the other way.

ELEANOR. I'm sure he doesn't mean to be cruel.

JAMES. If I came with you, I'd only have to walk all the way back before I could start my walk.

NELL. Yes, of course.

She has joined him at the front door, which he opens.

ELEANOR. I don't think we can blame him for having a selfish nature.

JAMES (*kissing her*). See you later.

ELEANOR. This incident as I left to come here —

NELL. Have a nice walk.

They go out. JAMES shuts the door. We see their silhouettes going off opposite ways. ELEANOR turns back to the DOCTOR.

ELEANOR. — gives you an idea what I mean. He set off positively
enough, it's a chilly day, but I couldn't help seeing how soon
he slowed down and seemed to be hovering. I didn't look
back till I reached the main road near the station. Our house is
easy to see from there and I took in something with half a
mind that only really dawned when I was halfway here in
the train. Our car had gone.

Music. Lights change.

*JAMES opens the front door again, comes in, looks about,
beckons to the same GIRL, who follows, looking about
again as though she'd never seen the house before.*

*When lights return on NELL, ELEANOR has gone. NELL
is seated, as before.*

Music ends.

NELL (*to the* DOCTOR): I've used most of my pills, by the way.
Can you give me another prescription?

*JAMES caresses the GIRL, leads her to the stairs, as before,
and up, making love all the way.*

*The DOCTOR writes again and hands NELL the paper,
standing between her and the living-room.*

They don't stop dreams, of course, but they help me sleep.
Are there any pills to banish day-dreams?

*JAMES leads the GIRL to the bedroom. Music. NELL
remains watching them but the DOCTOR goes off.*

*Above, lights on private view area as a screen is turned to
admit a WOMAN ASSISTANT in a dress shop.
She brings clothes on her arm, hangs them on a frame, turns
other screens, revealing mirrors.*

*ELEANOR and KATE follow her on, as the bedroom door
closes on JAMES and the GIRL.*

*KATE and ELEANOR talk privately while the ASSISTANTS
busy about.*

KATE. So you think he'd waited till he thought you were out of
sight then driven off in the car to see *her*?

ELEANOR. I do, yes, but the doctor's suggestion was that
James had realised he'd been unkind and driven the car all
round the common looking for me to give me a lift to the
station.

KATE. And hadn't found you?

ELEANOR. That was his suggestion.

KATE. Sounds reasonable.

ELEANOR. A belated kindness, yes, it does. Except that when
I got back two hours later the car still wasn't there and nor
was he.

KATE. What did he say when he *did* come in?

The ASSISTANT *shows them the clothes they've chosen and*
KATE *begins to change.*

ELEANOR. He said he'd been to buy some materials. And
showed me the paints and brushes. Trouble is, the supplier's
only ten minutes away.

KATE. If I were you, I'd turn a blind eye. He feels spied on, you
learn nothing, he can lie. It's useless. Somewhere I heard this
great saying. Love isn't 'Where've you been?', it's 'hullo'.

ELEANOR. That's all right for a sexy affair. But what about
afterwards?

KATE. Does there have to be any afterwards?

ELEANOR. Marriage, for instance.

KATE *has been changing into the underwear.* NELL *is*
climbing the stairs, but mostly hidden in half-light.

KATE. Ah well, I wouldn't know.

ELEANOR. You lived with Albert for five years.

KATE. Living with is different.

ELEANOR. Is it?

KATE (*displaying herself*). What d'you think?

ELEANOR. It's very you.

NELL (*appearing*). How could James have touched that
repulsive flesh?

ELEANOR. But our taste's very different. I couldn't wear it.

NELL. And if I did, James hates all that bordello tat.

ELEANOR. If it's the kind of thing your lover likes —

NELL. Right.

ELEANOR. I should buy it.

> KATE *still considers herself in the glass.* ELEANOR's *trying on the negligee.*

NELL. You're an anthology of all James said he hated. Your smell, your complexion, the texture of your hair —

KATE. Trying on new clothes is life's greatest pick-me-up.

ELEANOR. Why d'you need a pick-me-up? I thought you were in love.

KATE (*shrugs*). Love's never easy. Unlike sex.

> The ASSISTANT *shows in another* WOMAN *to try on clothes.*

NELL. Sex easy? You're talking like a man. *For* a man. Talk to *me*.

KATE. Don't misunderstand. It's not easy deceiving wives, for instance. Especially when they're friends, like you. Not pleasant either.

ELEANOR. Then why go for middle-aged husbands?

KATE. They're wittier, more interesting, they've done something with their lives.

NELL. And aren't so demanding sexually?

KATE. And as lovers they take their time. This does nothing for me.

> JIM *has come into the living-room.* NELL *moves across the balcony to the other side.* JIM *has the Christ painting in its frame.*
> KATE *changes again, tries the next garment.* ELEANOR *looks at herself.*

JIM. Eleanor, love, time's running out. You and I have twenty,

twenty-five years, if we're lucky, slowing down like a rusty motor till one day we stop forever. So this is probably my last chance and where's the harm? It's marvellous being a lover. You remember that from all those men before we married?

He leaves the painting and goes off to the music-room.

NELL *is joined by* AGNES *carrying two drinks. Around them stand a crowd of men with drinks, talking to each other.*

AGNES. See if that helps.

NELL *has taken pills from her handbag and now swallows one with the drink.*

NELL. I thought I was going mad. They told me it was a symptom of the menopause.

AGNES. Who did?

NELL. The doctors.

AGNES. All men?

NELL. Yes.

AGNES. They're everywhere.

They drink.

ELEANOR. The fact I'm suspicious he's got another woman doesn't mean he has. It just means I'm suspicious.

NELL. The more I asked him, the more he hated me.

AGNES. Well, he *would.*

KATE. Do what I did with Albert. Make him suspicious of you.

ELEANOR. Mistrusting each other hasn't been our way.

KATE. It seems to be now.

ELEANOR. And who's fault's that?

KATE. Good question.

She again displays different underwear for the glass.

JAMES *enters from the music-room with some polythene and sticky tape. During the next scene he studies the painting and prepares the wrapping.*

KATE. Does anything particularly make you doubt him?

ELEANOR. Oh, no, a million signs. Either he talks too little or too much. He skulks about as though he's in a mystery. I find cigarette-ends in the ashtray of the car and neither of us smokes. The last few weeks there are several hours I can't account for, no matter how many questions I ask. He makes calls from publix boxes, while he's supposed to be jogging.

KATE. Don't tell me you spy on him?

ELEANOR. I can hear the ten-pence pieces clinking in his track-suit pocket.

The ASSISTANT *returns with another customer who tries on clothes behind another screen.*
ELEANOR *displays the negligee and* KATE *another.*

JIM. I've inspired love. That's my trouble. I'm an unemotional man who's inspired a passion in my partner. And I needn't tell you what passion means? Suffering. Self-inflicted torture. Masochism. All that's holy. Like that exquisite depiction of a bleeding corpse that's waiting for me in Zurich. By day I'll patch up the blood and freshen the wounds where they've lost their brilliance over the years but every night I'll fuck as though life depended on it. Which, of course, it does.

KATE (*looks at herself*). Now that looks more like a dirty week-end in Morocco. Don't you think?

ELEANOR. Oh, yes. And how about this for Florence?

KATE. For anywhere. I knew that was you somehow.

ELEANOR. But hell's bells, look at the price.

The ASSISTANT *has come over.*

KATE. I'll take this one.

The ASSISTANT *smiles and collects other clothes.*

ELEANOR. Well, *I* like it but will my hubby?

KATE. I should think so.

ELEANOR. In that case I'll risk it then. (*To the* ASSISTANT:) Because if she doesn't know, who does?

KATE *laughs.*

The ASSISTANT *looks at each of them, takes the gown, goes to attend the other customer.*

KATE *and* ELEANOR *put on dresses.*

How long you going to be in Morocco?

KATE. Three days. Just enough to freshen my fading tan.

ELEANOR. We're having a *week* in Florence, though not till after Christmas. He'll be working on a Crucifixion in Switzerland for a few days soon and I wanted to go with him. He said it would be all work and no play and I accused him of lying and taking his floozie instead —

KATE. It doesn't sound like a load of laughs, I must say —

ELEANOR. — so, to allay my suspicions perhaps, he's booked this week beside the Arno.

KATE. Well, out of you and the floozie, I know who's got the best of the bargain.

ELEANOR. It's where we went on our honeymoon.

KATE. Out of Florence and Zurich, I know where I'd rather go.

They continue dressing.

Other doors open and NELL *and* AGNES *step out.*

A silhouette appears at the front door downstairs. JAMES *takes the painting to it and opens to admit a* PORTER, *carrying a large canvas, its front upstage, wrapped in polythene.*

The PORTER *asks* JAMES *to sign an invoice and goes, taking the Christ.*

NELL. In the ordinary way I might not have noticed.

AGNES. How d'you mean, the ordinary way?

NELL. Before suspicion became a way of life.

ELEANOR. Did I say Zurich?

KATE. What?

ELEANOR. I didn't mention Zurich.

KATE. Didn't you? Oh. (*She moves towards the* ASSISTANT.) I'll pay for that in cash.

ELEANOR. I didn't say he was going to Zurich. (KATE, *the* ASSISTANT *and the* CUSTOMER *look at her. She shouts*:) I said Switzerland.

KATE. So?

The ASSISTANT *goes, with* KATE.

ELEANOR. How did you know it was Zurich? Who's told you if it wasn't me? Don't think you can just walk off without explaining how you knew . . .

AGNES. I thought you knew it was still going on.

The CUSTOMER *follows* KATE.

ELEANOR. Did you hear what I said? Kate! Wait for me! (*She follows them off.*)

NELL *and* AGNES *move along the upper level.*

AGNES. You must be the last person in London to find out.

NELL. She told me there was another man.

AGNES. *One* another?

NELL. One special man she met in America and fell in love with.

AGNES. Is that what she said? Well, it didn't last long. He was the usual middle-aged man with the usual wife but with this one unusual feature — he preferred the wife to Kate. After a week or two he wrote and told her so.

NELL. How d'you know all this?

AGNES. I make it my business to know about her.

NELL. Why didn't you tell *me*?

AGNES. It never occurred to me you needed telling. They were at Private Views together, sales at Sotheby's.

NELL. I knew there was someone. Her I somehow never guessed at.

AGNES. Well, at least you hadn't got your faith back. That's a sign of growing awareness. Faith is a luxury you can't afford now. Or ever again. What did she say after you caught her out?

NELL. Walked straight from the shop and into a cab that happened to be standing there. That was the reason I came round to you. You were the only person I could turn to.

AGNES. My dear, you should have asked me sooner.

NELL. I was afraid it was only inside here. He's almost convinced me I was going mad.

AGNES. I heard he'd sent you to the shrink.

NELL. Is there anything you don't know?

AGNES. The same one Albert sent me to. Their old chum Michael at the Middlesex sends all the psychologically battered wives to him. It's part of the male conspiracy.

NELL. James even pretended that he didn't like me going there.

AGNES. Eleanor, love, it's time you listened to the hooker's war-cry: don't take it lying down.

NELL *moves across to the stairs.*

Downstairs JAMES *stands upstage looking at the canvas.*

ELEANOR *enters at the front door, looks at him, then the picture. She carries a bag from the dress shop.*

JAMES. Hello, love. How was your afternoon? You'll be glad to hear old killjoy's gone and look what they've brought instead.

He leans the picture, face upstage, goes to music-room. She goes to cupboard, hangs her coat. NELL *is now with her.*

NELL. All right, is it decided? Do we tell him to go?

ELEANOR. And if he does?

NELL. We must learn to forget him.

ELEANOR. I can't forget him. He's half my life.

NELL. Imagine him dead. Then you'd have to.

ELEANOR. Albert's dead, Agnes never forgets him long.

NELL. Kate's forgotten him already.

ELEANOR. She's twenty-five, there's time for her. Ten years ago when Richard wanted me, I could have tried a fresh start.

JAMES returns with a bradawl and scissors and begins to unfix the staples on the wrapping. ELEANOR and NELL are at the other side of stage.

NELL. Richard was a romantic bachelor. He was into celibacy as James is into fornication. He kept himself at such a level of anguish that sex could only have been a let-down.

ELEANOR (*smiling*). An anti-climax!

NELL (*laughing*). An anti-climax!

JAMES hears none of this.

JAMES. Been shopping?

ELEANOR. Yes, with Kate.

JAMES. How is she? Still in love?

ELEANOR. Oh, yes.

NELL. Richard 'courted' you, didn't he? With flowers —

ELEANOR. And respectful ways and passionate language —

NELL. Such a change from James who used to describe himself sexually as a 'straight up and away man'.

She looks across at him.

How appetising can you get!

ELEANOR. And quibbling over the word 'love', grousing when I had the curse —

She looks at the nightdress she's bought —

NELL. Frowning at Richard's expensive roses —

ELEANOR (*imitating* JAMES): 'Extravagant spending money like that when the garden's full of daffodils — '

NELL (*laughing*). Explaining those roses became a way of life — I had to ask him not to buy them.

JAMES. Ah. That what you've bought?

ELEANOR. A nightdress, yes, for the week in Florence.

JAMES. Must have cost the earth.

NELL. Poor Richard said 'I can never take you away, or buy you clothes or wine or roses — what can I do to express my love?'

ELEANOR (*turning back to her*). And soon after that gave me an ultimatum. Either/or.

NELL. Like you're going to give James.

ELEANOR. What else can I do? How can I keep him?

NELL. Share him. Let him go to Zurich.

ELEANOR. Perhaps she'll disappoint him?

NELL. Now come on, Eleanor, have some pride.

ELEANOR. What's pride matter?

JAMES. This is going to be a swine. Matching this colour.

He turns the unwrapped painting so that we see the whole area is covered uniformly with yellow acrylic. He looks closely at one patch.

That watermark there, you see?

But she isn't looking. He carries the picture off through the kitchen door.

NELL (*packing the nightdress into the bag*). Tell him he's free to go to Zurich but not come back. Or stay with me and give her up. But no more lies!

ELEANOR. All right.

NELL. And don't let him dodge again.

ELEANOR. I won't.

NELL. He'll fog the issue if he can. It's in his interest to keep you both —

JAMES returns without the picture, NELL breaks off, now on the stairs. She looks at ELEANOR. JAMES smiles, turns to pour a drink.

JAMES. Did Kate buy anything?

ELEANOR. A nightdress.

JAMES. Pretty tarty, I'll bet?

ELEANOR. You'll be able to judge when you get to Zurich. Only if you go, don't bother coming back. I shan't be here.

NELL, *satisfied, continues up the stairs and into the bedroom.* JAMES *turns and is about to speak.*

I know all about it from Kate. All I have to say is: if you go, you'll be leaving me.

JAMES. I've never wanted to.

ELEANOR. Is that because she isn't any good in bed? That's what you said last time you finished with her. Not sensual.

JAMES. Not sensual the way you are, no. Something a bit implausible. Sexy without sensuality.

ELEANOR. Sexy? I see.

JAMES. Automatic. The price of changing partners so often is that you have to become a soloist.

ELEANOR. You love her. You're describing her with love! Whenever we've had sex lately, you've talked about her immediately after. Oh, Christ, that should have told me.

JAMES. I don't know what is meant by love. I never have. What I feel for her is sexual attraction. Pure and simple.

ELEANOR. That's what men want to hear. Pornography. No periods. No pregnancy. No growing fond. No consequences. Violence without bruises.

JAMES. It's a physical act. It can be at its best between two people who don't even know each other's names.

ELEANOR. You've known each other's names for years.

JAMES. We've tried not to let that matter. We *enjoy* it.

ELEANOR. She enjoys you. She enjoys the power she has over you. And indirectly over me.

JAMES. She hasn't any power over me.

ELEANOR. Then give her up. You can't. You went on seeing
her after you swore you wouldn't.

NELL *comes from the bedroom in a nightdress, followed by*
JIM *in pyjamas.*

JIM. I *had* to swear. You put a gun to my head.

NELL. I offered you a choice.

JIM. All or nothing.

NELL. Her or me.

JIM. You knew I wouldn't give you up.

NELL. You love *her*, why shouldn't you? She's young, available —

JIM. I've already said I don't know what love means. Except pain
and trouble and ownership. But you and I have been together
twenty-five years. Two daughters and a string of flats and
houses, annual holidays, narrow escapes. God-knows-how-
many orgasms.

NELL. You make me sound like a family album. Whereas for
Kate you feel desire, fascination —

JIM. I enjoyed the newness of her, yes. The flattery, the danger.
At a time our life had grown secure and predictable, she
brought back drama, looks across crowded rooms.

JAMES. Whenever I saw men touch her, I was elated because I'd
been there.

ELEANOR. All the other ageing husbands?

NELL. Not to mention arms dealers, property speculators,
journalists.

JIM. Abusing her doesn't help —

ELEANOR. That's not abuse. That's fact. She's essentially
uncreative.

JAMES. So am I.

ELEANOR. She'll never finish that book she's started.

NELL. She lacks the stamina.

JIM (*to* NELL): There are too many books in the world already.

Not to mention paintings and Passions and plays.

JAMES. Too much of everything. (*He goes about the room, indicating as he speaks.*) Too many chairs and tables —

JIM. — and curtains and carpets —

JAMES. Too much of all this clutter.

He throws some things about — cushions, magazines, paper flowers.

ELEANOR (*to* NELL): He didn't throw anything fragile.

NELL. I noticed that.

They laugh.

JAMES. I can't I'm too inhibited.

JIM. But she's got what I somehow never had — youth and independence.

NELL. I had that once. Until you turned me into a bourgeois wife, suffocated me with apparatus because it suited you.

JIM (*to* NELL): Then throw it all off. Be young again. She can help us. You must admit, love, bed's been much better lately.

JAMES (*to* JIM): The new flavour helped me relish the old.

ELEANOR (*to* NELL): The old!

NELL (*to* JIM): Get me a glass of Perrier.

ELEANOR. If she's so rejuvenating, you'd better go and live with her. Morning, noon and night.

JAMES. I don't want to.

ELEANOR. See how tasty you find her then.

JIM (*to* ELEANOR): Can you hear me? I don't want to. And even if I did, I doubt very much whether she'd want me.

NELL. Is that what's stopping you? Ah!

ELEANOR. Well, have no fears. She wants you all right.

NELL. She's wanted you from the day of Albert's funeral.

ELEANOR. If you think it's only your poor old cock she's

after, you're flattering yourself.

JIM *gives her a glass of water.*

NELL. She wants to take you away from me.

JAMES. I don't think we can ever know with her. She belongs to another generation — free of convention, independent —

NELL. Hah!

JAMES. One of the people men of my age wanted to create.

JIM. Yes, the freedom we advocated is the air they breathe.

NELL (*to* JIM): Her independence is based on daddy's tax — dodge trusts.

JAMES. She parks on double yellow lines, she walks straight to the head of queues, she grabs what's going —

ELEANOR. In other words, disregards the morality you've always lived by.

JAMES. I've been very moral, yes.

ELEANOR. So go to her. What's keeping you here?

JIM. You!

NELL. An old flavour?

JIM (*indicating the room*). This!

NELL. A prison?

JIM (*to* NELL): We need her, Eleanor. She can save us.

NELL. You can't have both.

JIM. Why not?

Pause.

He moves towards the door. They look at him.

I mean that. Why not?

He turns and goes from the room. NELL *follows into the hall as he climbs the stairs. The sense of place is re-established. She shouts upwards.*

NELL. Because I won't be second-best. Would you expect it? A

housekeeper whose husband keeps his love and desire for
another woman?

JIM (*shouting down*): It's half past two in the morning. If you
want me to go on with my moral working life tomorrow —

NELL. I don't!

JIM. — you'll have to let me get some sleep.

NELL. It's over, James. We're finished.

He goes into the bedroom, slamming the door.

*JAMES and ELEANOR watch NELL return to the living-
room. She takes out a bottle, shakes out a number of pills
into her hand and swallows them with the Perrier. She
chooses a record from stacked sleeves and puts it on the
player . . .*

JAMES (*to her, urgently*): This is a game!

ELEANOR (*to him*): A game?

JAMES. You must learn to play.

ELEANOR. You're a baby, James. You want to have your cake
and eat it.

JAMES. When I was a young man, cake was rationed.

Heavy rock music bursts out, fortissimo.

*NELL goes off to the kitchen while on other parts of the
stage the non-speaking actors appear wearing night-clothes.
They stand watching, having been awoken by the noise. They
complain to NELL and to each other.*

*JIM comes from the bedroom and down the stairs, running.
JAMES and ELEANOR watch. He gets to the player and takes
off the record with a violent screech of skidding stylus.*

*NELL reappears from the kitchen carrying a plastic bag full
of laundry, which she tips in a heap on the floor.*

JIM. You surely don't want the neighbours to suffer because
you and I — what's this?

NELL. Your lover's laundry.

JIM. What?

NELL. She had so much to do before her dirty week-end in Morocco and since leaving Albert's flat she'd had no washing machine so I offered to do it for her.

JIM. You what?

NELL. She'd been hoping to do it at the launderette but I said it was no trouble so she put it in the boot of *my* car and I was going to drop it off next time I went to the doctor —

JIM. You should never have made such an offer.

NELL. But now you can give it to her when you catch the plane for Zurich.

ELEANOR. I thought she was a friend. And Agnes too. You haven't left me any girl-friends.

NELL *throws articles of* KATE's *laundry at* JIM, *who tries to pick them up and return them to the bag.*

NELL. These childish socks! This sequinned blouse! These frilly knickers! Hasn't she got filthy taste?

JIM. She's different, that's all.

NELL (*showing him her clothes*). You don't agree? You don't agree that's awful?

JAMES. Yours isn't the only way of dressing.

JAMES *helps him clear up.*

NELL (*to* JIM): A year ago you would have.

JIM. You shouldn't have done this —

NELL. Now you can only think of the times you took them off, I suppose — revealing that repulsive flesh of hers —

She attacks him with her fists, pounding at his chest and shoulders as he turns away to avoid her blows. He falls down and she kicks at him with her bare feet.

JAMES *and* ELEANOR *and all the neighbours watch in silence till she tires.*

JIM *stands, holding her.*

JIM. All right, you win. I'll go tomorrow. You won't be happy till I do. Tonight I'll sleep in another room and tomorrow I'll go. Later on we'll sort out what to do about the paintings in my workshop . . . and all the rest of it . . .

NELL. Yes.

Pause. They stand exhausted.

JIM. Is that all right?

NELL. It's what you want.

Pause.

JIM. If you say so.

She goes upstairs. He starts picking up KATE's *clothes from about the room, stuffs them into the bag.*

NELL *goes to the small W.C. and pours a glass of water, takes out the bottle of pills.*

ELEANOR. Go and help.

JAMES. It had to come, some push from someone.

NELL *is swallowing the whole bottle of pills, one by one, with water.*

JIM. We can't go back to the old life now.

ELEANOR. Only thinking about yourself.

JAMES (*pointing upstairs*). You mean you're not?

JIM. I don't want to leave her but life's so short.

JAMES (*to* ELEANOR): Look how suddenly Albert died.

JIM. What's kindness and decency and loyalty going to matter then?

JAMES. In the endless night when no-one screws!

ELEANOR (*of* JIM). Why doesn't he know what's happening?

JAMES. Because I'd never do that. Not for you or Kate or the children.

ELEANOR *moves to appeal to the onlookers.*

ELEANOR. Help us, someone.

JAMES (*in the hall, looking up*). I lack the passion.

JIM *takes the bag of clothes to the kitchen. The onlookers go.*

NELL *finishes the pills and comes to the upper landing, drowsily. She sits on the top step.*

Pause.

JIM *returns to the hall, looks up to see* NELL *sitting there.*

JIM. Ah, listen, why don't you stay in our bed? I'll have Ruth's old room. That will give us a night's sleep, or what's left of it. We'll need clear heads tomorrow to discuss the question of our joint account and the credit cards and how to divide the spoils. You'll need the car, I'll use the train. Or perhaps I can take one of the girls' old bikes. You'll have to pass on messages from the answering machine.

ELEANOR. You looked free at last.

JAMES. I was frightened.

JIM. See how we've become an institution? The house, the girls, the pension fund —

JAMES. A whole political structure.

ELEANOR. Blow it up. Thousands do.

NELL. I should have thought of this sooner. So much simpler for everyone. You could keep this place, she could move in with you . . .

JIM. What? You're mumbling rather . . .

NELL. And I'd be free of both of you. All of it . . .

JIM. Well, when I go you will be, yes . . .

He is at the bottom of the stairs.

NELL. I love my children . . . tell them I love them . . .

She stands, loses balance and falls down several stairs till JIM *saves her.*

JIM. What's the matter with you?

NELL. The sleeping tablets.

JIM. No. Oh, no.

He holds her face and looks at it. Her eyes are closed.

How many?

NELL. Mm?

JIM. How many did you take?

NELL. The whole lot.

JIM. How many's that?

NELL. I don't know.

JIM. Think.

NELL. I stopped counting at thirty.

JIM. Stand up. Come on, stand.

He pulls her to her feet and unsteadily helps her up the stairs and into the W.C. He lets her collapse on her knees in front of the lavatory and then sticks two fingers into her mouth. She makes retching sounds and he holds her head over the pedestal but she does not vomit. He tries again. She protests and tries to push his hand away.

JIM. You've got to. Come on.

ELEANOR. We'd been looking forward to this for years.

JAMES. What?

ELEANOR. Being at home together. Just the two of us.

They are standing downstage looking up at NELL and JIM as NELL again makes retching noises.

ELEANOR. What did you feel for me?

JAMES. At this moment? Let me think . . .

ELEANOR. Love?

JAMES. Christ, no! Hadn't we had enough of love? It was love that brought us to that!

He points to the scene above.

ELEANOR. What then?

JAMES. Amazement, I think.

ELEANOR. Why?

JAMES. That you could have tried to take the only life you'll ever have.

Retch.

JIM. That's a good try . . . but I don't think you've brought up anything . . . come on now . . . up on your feet . . .

NELL. Leave me alone . . .

He helps her as they leave the lavatory for the stairs.

ELEANOR. Why amazed? I'd lost your love. I'd nothing to live for.

JIM. We're going downstairs to ring the doctor . . . try to concentrate on walking . . .

JAMES. I thought we agreed we'd never loved.

ELEANOR. But now I realised we had.

NELL *tries to sit on the stairs but* JIM *keeps her walking.*

JIM. Don't depend on me.

ELEANOR. All the time. Without knowing it.

JIM. That's a good girl.

ELEANOR. In this game, as you call it, I had no cards left to play.

JIM (*as they reach the lower level and the sofa*): Now where's the telephone? Tell me where it is.

ELEANOR. Except my life.

JIM. What's the doctor's number? Try to remember, head up, tell me the doctor's number.

ELEANOR *goes.* JAMES *moves after her some paces, speaking to her.*

JAMES. More than amazement I felt anger. That you'd yet again held a gun to my head.

NELL. . . . the front of the book?

JIM. I know but try to remember it. Concentrate.

He finds the number and dials while NELL *mumbles.*

JAMES (*returning to look down at* NELL). I'll show you how much I love you . . . I'll tell myself I'll die for you. Which may well ruin the rest of *your* life too . . . '

JIM. Doctor? Sorry. James Croxley here . . .

JAMES. Of course I prayed to the god I don't believe in that you wouldn't die.

JIM. Very urgent, yes, I'm afraid my wife's taken an overdose . . .

JAMES. Or survive with a damaged brain.

JIM. Over thirty. We're not really sure.

JAMES. I imagined you dead and as a hopeless cripple and none of that made me love you either.

JIM. What can I do until you get here?

JAMES. You'll never know this, Eleanor, but as I saw you lying there I hated you. For the first and last time.

JIM. All right, doctor, thank you.

He puts down the phone. Pulls NELL *to her feet.*

Come on, my dear —

JAMES. No pangs of guilt. Why should I? It wasn't my fault.

JIM. Now make an effort to stand upright.

JAMES. I don't want anyone to die for love of me.

He goes. Lights on JIM *and* NELL.
He has moved her to the stairs.

JIM. We're going to climb the stairs again now. Then we may come down them again because you mustn't fall asleep before the doctor gets here.

He gets her to the stairs and up they go again.

He says you'll be all right. It takes half an hour for barbiturates to get into the blood-stream. So, though it was a stupid thing to do, you weren't in danger as long as you let me know in time. Which you did.

On upper level, he walks her along, back and forth.

Someone told me most women who try to kill themselves don't succeed. Whereas most men do. Did you know that?

NELL. Who?

JIM. What?

NELL. Who told you that? Was it Michael at the Middlesex?

They go as the lights go.

Christmas music. A choir singing 'In The Bleak Midwinter'.

Lights come up slowly on the living-room. Outside snowy scenes. A YOUNG WOMAN is decorating with tinsel and paper chains. ELEANOR comes in from the bedroom, doing the same upstairs.

A YOUNG MAN comes from the kitchen bringing a Christmas tree in a tub. He stands it in the living-room and begins to add bells, lights, etc.

ELEANOR has come downstairs and the YOUNG WOMAN has gone to the kitchen. The YOUNG WOMAN returns with a tray of wine glasses, poured ready for guests. ELEANOR's cleared up the bits into a box and gives it to the YOUNG MAN.

JAMES comes from the kitchen bringing the yellow canvas. JIM is with him. The other three make welcoming noises.

ELEANOR takes two glasses of wine for herself and JAMES, the young people too. JAMES leans the picture against the back wall and takes the glass. They raise their glasses. Music ends.

ELEANOR. Happy Christmas.

THE OTHERS. Happy Christmas.

They drink. NELL comes on upstairs and watches from the balcony.

JAMES. And the painting's finished.

ELEANOR. Oh, well done.

JAMES. As near as I can get. That yellow was a swine to
match. Acrylics are always tricky.

They all look at the canvas.

ELEANOR. It looks exactly the same to me but I couldn't even
see a stain.

They laugh.

How did you know it was there?

JAMES. It was there all right. Stood out a mile if you're used to
looking at paintings.

NELL. You mean, like her?

ELEANOR. It may be philistine but I always say I could do those
paintings with a roller.

JAMES. I know you do.

He kisses her affectionately. The YOUNG WOMAN *has fetched
snacks.*

NELL. Is that something else you shared? An appreciation of
minimal art? Something you discussed between bangs?

ELEANOR. Well, now you've done you can give a hand here.

NELL. A post-coital seminar topic?

JAMES. Absolutely.

NELL. The meaning of the all-yellow canvas?

ELEANOR. We're a bit behind so hang some mistletoe and
holly.

JAMES. Right.

ELEANOR. You and Robert can go and dress now. Your father
and I can finish here.

The two go upstairs while JAMES *gets out holly and mistletoe
and a step-ladder to hang it.*

ELEANOR *goes to the kitchen.* JIM *is on the other side of
the stage.* NELL *remains on the upper level watching the men.*

JAMES *climbs the steps.* JIM *takes out an air-mail envelope, unfolds a letter inside, scans it.*

JIM. 'Dearest Kate, I picked up your latest letter from the gallery. If they'd known how indendiary it was, they might have called the fire brigade'.

NELL. This isn't any good, is it? Nothing's settled, nothing's changed.

JIM. 'Getting it home nearly burnt a hole in my pocket'.

NELL. I'm not allowing it to drift like this. But you won't stop it, will you? You can't, it's beyond you . . .

JIM. 'I envy you spending this time of year in The Holy Land, where Christmas isn't celebrated. I'm told you'll see nothing of it, if you avoid Manger Square in Bethlehem'.

NELL. Giving isn't in your nature. That's a terrible misfortune and I'm sorry for you.

JIM. 'Eleanor's still got a way to go before I've nursed her back to health'.

NELL. I offered you everything I had but you couldn't respond . . .

JIM. 'She won't go back to the shrink. Several times a week we're up all night . . . '

NELL. Poor baby!

JIM. 'Obviously I can't risk hurting her so till she's well again, we'll have to make do with letters . . . '

NELL. You can't grow. You dream of change but when the chance comes you flirt with both —

JIM. ' . . . and while yours are as hot as the last, I shan't grumble . . . '

He takes out a crumpled air-letter, looks at it.

'The story of your international incident almost blew my head off . . . '

NELL. You're not even promiscuous. It's always the same girl, over and over . . .

ELEANOR *comes back with more trays for the party, sets them down.*

JIM. 'It gained an extra erotic charge by taking place near the sea at Galilee . . . '

ELEANOR. How are you getting on with the mistletoe?

JAMES (*climbing down*). What d'you *think*?

ELEANOR. Well, it's *sparing*, isn't it?

JAMES. Is it?

ELEANOR. Minimal. Like the painting.

NELL. Like you. Minimal man.

JAMES. Another bit of paganism swallowed up by Christmas. Let's try it, shall we?

They stand beneath the mistletoe, embrace and kiss.

JIM. 'I keep imagining I'm one of those Israeli soldiers. Either one who found you freshining the tail-end of your tan among the rocks. Or his mate who kept a watch on the road and the pair of you at the same time . . . '

He reads KATE's *letter to himself, avidly.*

NELL. But where are you? Out to lunch as usual.

JAMES. It seems to work.

ELEANOR. Yes?

NELL. No-one home.

JAMES. I think we can make a go of it, don't you?

NELL. No.

ELEANOR. We can try.

JIM puts away KATE's *letter.*

JIM. 'I want you both. I like how it was before but she wants all or nothing.'

NELL. I want a lover, not an old friend.

ELEANOR. Now you've ruined my face. And guests are due.

They separate. She goes off to the music-room. He clears up, takes things off to the kitchen.

NELL. You can't do without all this. A home, a place to work. But I can. Change doesn't frighten me. Once I'd lost your love, there was nothing to keep me here . . . so goodbye . . .

JIM. Love's a terrible thing. Of course it means anything you want it to but I mean the kind that kills. So let's not either of us ever mention the word again . . .

NELL goes off to the bedroom as JAMES reappears and puts on a record. JIM folds and seals his letter in the envelope.

The door bell rings as NELL continues to climb. ELEANOR comes from the music-room and opens the door to AGNES.

AGNES. Happy Christmas!

ELEANOR' Happy Christmas!

They embrace as JAMES starts a record of choristers singing another carol. The two YOUNG PEOPLE return from upstairs as NELL goes into the bedroom. ELEANOR shuts the door behind AGNES and helps her off with her outer clothes. They go together into the living-room, where JAMES embraces AGNES. The YOUNG PEOPLE join them and they all get drinks. The doorbell rings and JAMES goes to open it to a MIDDLE-AGED COUPLE bearing gifts. He lets them in and shuts the door. Same process as with AGNES, joining the party in the living-room. The young WOMAN opens to the next arrivals. We hear their festive chatter and the bell ringing at intervals.

Then the bell rings and no-one hears, except JIM. He has remained in the hall and now opens the door to KATE. NELL comes from the bedroom carrying a small case. JIM and KATE embrace. He unbuttons her fur coat and gazes at her body beneath. NELL gets her coat, puts it on in the hall while JIM goes down in front of KATE. NELL leaves by the front door.

The party continues, spilling into the hall as others arrive. Of course nobody sees JIM and KATE.
The singing swells.